MAJORING
IN
LAW

MAJORING
IN
LAW

It's Not Right for Everyone.
Is It Right for You?

STEFAN UNDERHILL

WITH CHARLOTTE MORRISSEY

Series editor: Carol Carter

THE NOONDAY PRESS
Farrar, Straus and Giroux
New York

LIBRARY OF CONGRESS CATALOGING-IN-PUBLICATION DATA
Underhill, Stefan.
Majoring in law : It's not right for everyone.
Is it right for you? / Stefan Underhill. — 1st ed.
p.   cm.
Includes bibliographical references.
1. Law—Vocational guidance—United States.   2. Practice of law—
United States.   I. Title.
KF297.U53   1995
340'.023'73—dc20   95-11395 CIP

FOR MARIAH, MARK, DEVIN, KERRY,
KENT, AND MEREDITH
Follow your dreams, kids

ACKNOWLEDGMENTS

This book would never have been written without Charlotte Morrissey. Long before I did, Charlotte recognized the need for a book to challenge would-be lawyers to undertake some serious self-reflection before committing themselves to law school. She did important early thinking about how to approach the subject, interviewed many of the lawyers quoted here, and helped me with the writing and editing. Charlotte not only convinced me to write this book in the first place, she also followed through with the frequent and enthusiastic pep talks necessary for me to complete it. For her insightful comments and faithful support I will be forever grateful.

Charlotte and I both thank our spouses, Mike Morrissey and Mary Pat Underhill, for their loving patience and personal sacrifice over the many months since this project began. This book was written during the countless weekends and evenings when Mary Pat and Mike took on more than their share of child care, newborn care, and household errands to free up time for us in front of our computer screens. Mary Pat has always been a source of strength and inspiration, and she provided both while I worked on this book.

There is a tremendous team standing behind these pages, to whom I owe much. Jessica Franken helped keep the book alive through the lean early days. Carrie Brandon cheerfully sought out interviews with lawyers I would never have found. Carol Carter's encouragement, patience, and stamina led to the series of career books of which this is just one. Her efforts paved the way for me and others. Elisabeth Kallick Dyssegaard edited with a firm but gentle hand, improving my writing without squeezing my personality out of it.

This book is the product of more than those who wrote it, edited it, and produced it. It captures the thoughts and words of many lawyers. Some are quoted and some are named—but many who spoke to Charlotte and me are not. To all who shared their time, their experiences, and their often very personal feelings about the law, I send my warmest thanks.

S.U.
Fairfield, Connecticut
July 13, 1995

CONTENTS

MAJORING
IN
LAW

INTRODUCTION

TO BE OR NOT
TO BE A LAWYER

You can't decide. Some days the idea of going to law school seems like a no-brainer. Other days you have those nagging doubts. Are you ready for three more years of school? Maybe not, but being a student can't be any worse than facing the real world. You're only twenty-one, you've got the rest of your life to work. Still, if you started a job now, you'd be three years ahead of the game *and* you'd save yourself fifty or sixty thousand dollars in tuition and living expenses. Better to be making money than taking on more student loans, right? But if you get one of those high-paying jobs at a big-city law firm after law school, you could probably pay off your loans in no time. . . .

You can't decide. The job you're in now seems like a dead end. It pays the bills, but by Tuesday you're looking forward to the weekend. Doing the same thing day after day has gotten to be so *boring*. Law is exciting. Lawyers get to think about stimulating ideas all the time. You see lawyers on TV and read about them in the newspaper every day. But do you really want to go back to school? You've gotten pretty used to having that steady paycheck, and you're up for a promotion next year. If you become a lawyer it means starting all over again. . . .

You can't decide. Going back to school now that the kids are older sounds like it would be really stimulating. You've survived the diapers and car pool routine. Being PTA president was challenging, yet it wasn't like being out in the working world, earning a salary. It's time to stand up and be counted. But you haven't picked up a serious book for years, much less tried to pull all-nighters cramming for exams. Besides, it's not going to be easy to squeeze an expensive professional education into the household budget. . . .

You can't decide. That's why you picked up this book, right? To help you decide whether to go to law school, whether to become a lawyer. And to help get your future legal career off to a good start.

3

The indecision you feel about law now will actually help you decide whether law is right for you. Too few of the people who head off to law school each year have a clear vision of why they are going and what they hope to do when they get out. Unlike so many others, you will ask yourself some important questions *before* committing yourself. You'll end up truly deciding what's best for you.

This book is meant to help you help yourself. Make you question your assumptions. Make you do some homework. Make you think about whether or not law is the right career for you. If you ask yourself and others hard questions about the practice of law now, you will reduce the risk of making a career mistake.

If you decide that you do want to become a lawyer, you'll benefit from some preparation now. Your legal opportunities will be greater if you take steps to prepare for law school, get into the best law school you can, do well there, and gain a sense of the type of job you really want —long before it's time to start sending out résumés.

The advice in this book isn't mine alone. You'll also hear from many other lawyers around the country. Lawyers from different backgrounds. Lawyers working in government, for corporations, in firms, and on their own. Lawyers proud to be helping others. Lawyers worn down by the demands and stresses of their jobs. Even lawyers who have left the profession altogether. I hope their stories help you understand both the promise of law and its pitfalls.

At times, doing the work necessary to improve your career decision making may seem tedious. But it's your life we're talking about here. It's worth the effort. So let's get started.

∎ I ∎

WHETHER TO BECOME A LAWYER

· 1 ·

FALSE STARTS

"Daddy, what do you do at work every day?" asks my seven-year-old, Mark.

Take and make a hundred phone calls. Read and puzzle over contracts, memos, purchase orders, letters, court decisions, statutes, and regulations. Predict what other people will do: judges, other lawyers, businesspeople, the government. Think about disputes and how to avoid or resolve them. Advise people and corporations on issues important to them. Write letters, research papers, and court arguments. Worry about getting all my work done, keeping my clients happy, getting my clients to pay, finding the next client, getting home for the big soccer game.

"I'm a lawyer," I respond.

"But, Daddy, what's a lawyer?"

Good question. Pause. "A lawyer is someone who helps people solve their problems."

"Oh."

I'm not sure the answer satisfied Mark—and it certainly didn't satisfy me. But it started me thinking. There are lots of people who don't really know what lawyers do. Yet many of those same people are off taking the LSAT and preparing to go to law school. It doesn't make much sense for anyone to go to law school if they can't answer some basic questions about their chosen future profession, including the question "What's a lawyer?"

What's a Lawyer?

There are over 865,000 lawyers in the United States, so there are probably at least 865,000 answers to the question "What's a lawyer?" What lawyers do is only part of the answer. There is also whom they do it with, whom they do it for, and the very personal why they do it.

The "with," the "for," and especially the "why" have all been shaped by how and why they got where they are. Yes, all lawyers came through college and law school. And all survived the bar exam—or exams. But that's not what I mean.

I mean whether they were pushed into law by a relative who is a lawyer. Or simply became infatuated with lawyers in movies and on television. Whether they always knew they wanted to be lawyers. Or, as is true for so many, they simply couldn't think of a better way to keep their options open.

Nothing Better to Do with the Rest of Your Life?

For every lawyer who always wanted to become a lawyer, I'll bet there are five who simply drifted into law. The course of least resistance. Law is an easy option, because it requires no special course of study in college. You can major in English or engineering, business or baroque music.

And, of course, law is perfect for those who just can't decide what to do with the rest of their lives. Law school offers three more years of school during which to figure out career interests. And a law degree won't necessarily restrict you to a particular career path. Law grads become lawyers, but they also become bankers, politicians, journalists, and teachers. So lots of law students end up in law school for no particularly good reason.

It's junior year. Your parents had raised polite questions about your plans during your freshman and sophomore years. Now their questions have become a bit more pointed. Then you get the call: What are you going to do with the rest of your life?

The pressure is getting to you. What *are* you going to do with the rest of your life? You never even took organic chemistry, so medical school is out. And you've never felt you had any business sense whatsoever.

Then it hits you. You can decide not to decide. Keep your options open. Postpone everything for three years. Just take the LSATs!

You survived the phone call from home. You survived the LSATs. You even survived junior year. But still you have doubts. What do lawyers do anyway? And would you like it? Are lawyers as bad as all those jokes? What if you hate law school?

Kids, Don't Try This at Home

I had my doubts about becoming a lawyer. I never admitted that to anyone—not even myself. But nothing else can explain the way I approached getting into law school.

Maybe I thought it would just *happen*. Things had always worked out well before. I had been student body president and valedictorian of my high school class. I had been accepted to the University of Virginia. My grades were good. My LSATs were good. Why should getting into a top law school be a problem?

October. I sent away for law school applications. Wow, they want a lot of information. I'll have to get right on that. Maybe next week.

December. It's been a while since I got those law school applications. Let's see—oh, good, the deadline isn't until February 16.

February 15, 2 a.m. (*after* the Valentine's party at the dorms). Application form in the typewriter: "Describe the qualities that you think will make you a good lawyer." "What has been your greatest challenge, and how did you overcome it?" "Write an essay on a subject of your choosing, not to exceed 250 words." (These people are *not* serious.) Later, at the Federal Express office, craving sleep: "I need to send this one overnight to Cambridge and this one overnight to New Haven. You're *sure* they'll arrive by tomorrow?"

I heard from Harvard almost immediately. "The check accompanying your application for admission to the Harvard Law School has been returned for insufficient funds. No further action will be taken by the admissions committee with respect to your application unless and until you provide us with a substitute check in the amount of $75.00." At this point, I should just save my money, right?

Time Out

The rejections came flying in. But maybe that was just the kick in the pants I needed. Always want what you can't have, and all that. No law school admissions committee was going to tell me smugly that I wasn't up to their standards and get away with it. Just wait till next year!

At the time, I was taking a course in constitutional law at the University of Virginia. I went from interested to involved. Did extra reading. Started speaking up in class. Made study charts of how the Supreme Court justices voted on different issues. At the end of the semester, I crushed the final and earned a future letter of recommendation.

Still, there was no law school waiting for me come fall. Out of necessity, I decided to get a job. But I wanted to find work that would have some connection with the law. It was time to learn a little something about my future profession.

First choice for my year "off" was a job on Capitol Hill as a legislative assistant to a congressman or senator. I think I wrote every single member of Congress. (There are 535 of them. Just signing those letters took forever.) And I followed up many with office visits—smiling at hundreds of receptionists whose primary responsibility was to keep job seekers like me from seeing anyone with authority to hire.

Nothing. So I moved away from the Hill to those who feed off of it: law firms. Suddenly, I was getting some interest. After several quick interviews, I accepted the highest-paying offer, and soon was making an extravagant $12,000 a year as a paralegal.

Fail, Abort, Retry

My year as a paralegal was an excellent experience. (More about that later.) But I knew from the start that this was just a way station on my journey to law school. I wanted to spend the year—on the job and off —improving my chances of getting in next time.

I decided to seek help from the source. I wrote to the Dean of Admissions at Yale Law School, my top choice.

Dear Dean Thomas,

I applied unsuccessfully for admission to the Law School this year. I have taken a position as a paralegal and would like to spend the coming year doing whatever it takes to improve my chances for admission next year.

Please let me know whether the admissions committee would look more favorably on my application if I took graduate school courses at night, wrote for academic journals, spent time assisting nonprofit organizations, or the like. Thank you for your time and advice. I very much look forward to hearing from you.

Sincerely,

Stefan Underhill

It seemed like forever before I got a response.

Dear Mr. Underhill,

Thank you for your interest in Yale Law School. I am sorry to inform you that once you have been rejected for admission by the Law School, you have virtually no chance of being admitted upon reapplication. It has happened before, and your chances would be improved if you won a Rhodes or Marshall Scholarship. But I would recommend that you attend another law school and attempt to transfer to Yale after a successful first year elsewhere. Best wishes for your future success.

Very truly yours,

Dean of Admissions

Oh, thank you for the advice. It's that easy. Just become a Rhodes Scholar. No problem.

All's well that ends well. I reapplied to Yale a few years later, Oxford diploma in hand, and was accepted. But still I arrived there without a clear sense of why I wanted to become a lawyer. There was nothing else I wanted to do more, but in retrospect that wasn't a good enough reason. I should have had a clearer set of goals to justify taking on debts that have required me to write checks every month for the past ten years to pay off my student loans.

Try Your Luck

I got lucky. Almost by accident, I ended up in a career that has been satisfying and challenging. However, I've watched many talented, bright attorneys become disillusioned or unhappy. Some have left the practice of law altogether. Others have not—though they'd probably be happier if they did.

Matthew Winter also got lucky—both in the way he got into law and the way he got out. "I got my undergraduate degree from Michigan. A BS in wildlife management. That's what some of my relatives said, it was b.s. 'What's a kid from Long Island doing with a degree in wildlife management?!' . . . For a lot of personal reasons, I decided to try ROTC. I got a full scholarship for the last three years of college and owed the Army four years after that." While in the military, Matt applied for the Army's program for funded legal education. He was chosen from among 800 applicants to become one of the twenty-five people a year that the military sends to law school.

After graduation, Matt became a military prosecutor. "My first-year criminal law instructor was one of the worst teachers I had in law school. But in the middle of my second year, I got an internship with the U.S. Attorney's office. Because I had a security clearance from my work in the Army, I was the only intern who could work on the organized crime or drug task forces. I had a great time working with the DEA and the FBI. Without question, I felt I was working for the right side." While he was stationed at Fort Dix, New Jersey, Matt prosecuted many criminal cases. "In my first three months on the job, I tried five cases. I didn't know I wanted to try cases, but I liked it." As a prosecutor, Matt tried homicides, rapes, child-abuse cases, larcenies, and maiming cases, among others.

As a military lawyer, Matt also negotiated large government contracts, and became editor of *The Army Lawyer* and the *Military Law Review*. He became a legal writing instructor and taught trial advocacy, legal research and writing, and client interviewing and counseling at the Judge

Advocate's General School on the grounds of the University of Virginia in Charlottesville. While there, he took courses at night and received a master's degree in law. At that point, "I was due for an overseas tour. My wife and I were tired of moving around and we thought we could have more rewarding careers on the outside. It was the end of my military commitment and I figured it was time either to leave or to commit to stay in for another twenty years."

He left the Army and joined a private firm as an associate. "When trying to figure out what to do, I decided to go with the biggest firm I could find. It was a way to keep my options open, but was a very agonizing decision because other firms offered me more credit for my military service and more money." After three years there, Matt left the firm and, to some extent, left the practice of law. "The best part of working for the firm was the quality of my cases. I learned a phenomenal amount. But the time demands and lack of time with my family took a toll. There were a lot of stresses caused by living in a high-cost area and not being compensated enough to live close to work, which meant less time with my family." Now Matt serves as vice president and chief ethics and corporate compliance officer for a life insurance company he came in contact with through his work at the law firm. He works now primarily as a businessman, not a lawyer.

Matt has filled a variety of roles as a lawyer: prosecutor, contract negotiator and drafter, teacher, editor, private law firm associate. If he had it to do over again, would he become a lawyer? "No. Although things have worked out very well for me, I think there is a large percentage of lawyers out there trapped doing things they don't like. Lawyers' work is extremely hard and often very tedious. People do it because they think they're getting compensated well, but businessmen do more interesting work and get better pay. The quality of life is tremendously better in business. In many ways, professionals get the short end of the stick."

Your career decision and satisfaction don't have to depend upon luck (either good or bad). But they may depend on hard work.

· 2 ·

THE WHY KNOT

This chapter will examine information critical to your career choice. But it will require some effort on your part. What? you think. I paid good money for this book and I have to *get involved*?

Yeah, I know. We all hate doing the things we ought to do. Like house-cleaning and writing thank-you notes. Faced with the realization that you *ought* to read on, the temptation to channel-surf suddenly becomes overwhelming.

Hang in there! Thinking hard about your future isn't always fun. But you have at least a vague interest in law as a career or you wouldn't be reading this book. Remember, a vague interest, like a little knowledge, is a dangerous thing. Unless you think hard about your future now, you may get stuck in a job you don't like.

Take Sarah Labensky, a professional baker and author in Phoenix, Arizona. Sarah was a lawyer for three years. She practiced labor law with a top-flight firm, working on landmark cases that made headlines in the newspapers. Everything law should be, right? Wrong. Sarah felt that she was being stifled in her job. Every day she faced conflict: with the opposing lawyers, with her clients, and often within the firm. "The worst part of it all was that I didn't always feel that I was on the right side. And yet here I was, spending fourteen hours a day trying to prove that my side's cause was legally correct."

Sarah grew unhappier as time went on. Finally, she decided to leave the law, despite the fact that she had no other career in mind. She took a variety of part-time jobs (including waiting on tables). Only then did she begin to ask herself hard questions about what career she wanted to pursue and why. Sarah ultimately chose culinary arts because it was creative, was free of conflict, and allowed room for autonomy. And she's been much happier ever since. "But the six-year detour I took in law school and practicing law was rough."

13

To avoid needless detours over rough roads, you need to do *your* hard thinking now. So pour yourself a heavily caffeinated drink. And push on.

Don't Just Do It

Many lawyers complain about their careers with the refrain "Why did I go to law school anyway?" Obviously, they know why they went. But the reasons they had for going weren't good reasons. What they expected to do with a law degree isn't what they find themselves doing out in the real world. I know how they feel.

As a kid, I was into math and science. I loved building things, figuring things out. For years I was sure I'd become an architect. But I became infatuated with something sexier. Politics.

I was in high school during the Watergate scandal and the last few years of the Vietnam War. What's more, I went to a high school in Richmond, Virginia, where a judge ordered kids from the other side of town bused to my school to desegregate it. Politics and the law were flung at us from the front page of each morning's newspaper. Politics and the law said I had to face the chance of getting drafted to fight in an unpopular war. Politics and law decided who I went to school with and thus who would become my friends. Politics and law seemed to affect so much of my everyday life.

Architecture could no longer compare with the sudden passion I felt for politics. There were no mathematically right and wrong answers in political debates. And that made each individual's role so much more significant. With a strong argument, I knew I could change people's minds. I wanted to practice the power of persuasion. I dreamed of serving in the U.S. Senate.

Who needed to think about the best career path? If I wanted to help write laws I had to go to law school. And so I considered nothing else. Yet by the time I graduated from law school, my desire for elective office had died. I was sure I would hate the lifestyle, the loss of privacy, the need to keep the constituency happy. (The questions about whether or not I'd inhaled.) Other things were more important to me: family, friends, balance in my life. I wonder now whether I would have chosen law school if I'd simply asked myself a few hard questions.

I must admit that I got a little lucky. My practice in the commercial litigation department of Connecticut's largest law firm has proven both challenging and satisfying. I enjoy my work and I enjoy my colleagues. But I interviewed many lawyers and ex-lawyers who weren't so lucky. Some have hopped from job to job within the legal profession, looking for a job they would like. Others have given up hope and are leaving or have left the law altogether. In fact, studies show that 25 percent of the lawyers who graduated from law school after 1989 are "seriously considering" leaving their jobs.

Those aren't great odds. But together we're going to take a hard look at why you're considering law, what it is that you're likely to do as a lawyer, and whether the profession is one you'll enjoy. If you decide law suits you, we'll consider how to improve your chances of landing a place at the right law school and later the right legal employer.

Why Not Dentistry?

First things first. Where did your interest in law come from? Did someone tell you that you'd make a good lawyer? That you ought to be a lawyer? That they wanted you to be a lawyer? Or did you come up with the idea yourself?

Leslie Davis, who used to practice with a large New York law firm and who now oversees litigation for a Fortune 500 company, never even considered being a lawyer until after college. "I got an undergraduate degree in philosophy and music. After college, I found myself trying to support both my husband and myself. He was still a student and I was becoming really frustrated with him because he seemed to have no interest in law or medical school. I had been raised to think that a husband should support his wife. So I kept telling him that we needed a professional in the family. Finally, he turned to me one day and said, 'Why don't *you* go to law school?' A light just went on in my head. Hey, I thought, I can do that."

Dan Rashin recalls that while in college he had definitely decided to go into business, but still somehow ended up in law. "I was at the career counseling office and the woman there asked me if I was going to take the LSATs. I told her that I didn't need to take them, I was going into business. She said that unless I was *sure* I would *never* go to law school, I should take the LSATs now because I would do better on them now than after being out of school for a while. I wasn't convinced, but finally decided to take the test because I couldn't face the fact that I might rule out a career." Dan did "wildly better" than he expected on the LSAT, but still wanted to go into business. He applied only to three top law schools and got into them all. "At the start of spring semester senior year I got this fat letter from Harvard. I decided I could either spend my last semester at college worrying about finding a job—or I could enjoy myself and then go to Harvard Law School." Faced with that choice, he was off to law school.

Many lawyers have followed their parents into the law. Some willingly, some not. There can be a good deal of subtle pressure when a parent wants his or her child to become a lawyer. Law may sometimes be "in the blood," but it isn't always.

Charlotte Morrissey's father told her as a child, "The law is the greatest of all the professions. You're constantly learning, you help people solve problems, you're never bored, and you're your own boss." She remembers that he told her she would make a fine lawyer and love the law. Others agreed. Teachers, counselors, and lawyers told Charlotte that she'd make a good lawyer. "I thought I could be a lawyer, other people thought I could be a lawyer, so I decided I *should* be a lawyer. My family and friends seemed content with, and even proud of, my career choice." But it wasn't the right choice. After three years of practice with a prestigious law firm, Charlotte left the profession altogether to become an editor for a college textbook company. "For me, it's a much better fit than law was. I'm constantly learning, I feel I'm helping people, and I'm more of my own boss than I was as an attorney."

Not all lawyer role models are relatives. I grew up with Perry Mason and *To Kill a Mockingbird*'s Atticus Finch. There have been many TV and movie lawyers since. *NYPD Blue* or *Law and Order* may have inspired you to think about law. A few years back, *L.A. Law* sparked a surge in law school applications. The camera lens can make law look sexy and glamorous.

And there are real-world role models: judges, prosecutors, or simply the lawyer who lives down the street. We may not know what these people really do day to day. Yet their image or standing in the community makes law seem attractive. I feel sure that publicity surrounding the O. J. Simpson prosecutors and defense lawyers will lead many young people into legal careers.

You may not have a role model at all. Maybe law just seems more interesting than what you've been doing. That's how things looked to Jane Lehman, who spent three years singing professionally with the Tanglewood Festival Chorus of the Boston Symphony Orchestra. "In order to do the singing I wanted to, I had to supplement my income with a lot of menial jobs that were not satisfying intellectually. I delivered singing telegrams for a year and gave radio traffic reports. I discovered that I was intellectually starved and wanted something that would challenge me. I might never have realized that if I hadn't scooped ice cream at a health-food store."

You may have gained your interest in law for all or none of these reasons.

Pull out a pencil or pen and write out your answers to these five questions. It's important to commit your answers to paper because I will ask you to look back at them later. Besides, it's harder to fudge an answer if you actually write it down.

1. Describe the first time you ever thought about being a lawyer. Don't just say how old you were. Consider what it was that motivated you to think about law. What were you doing? Most important, why did you have the thought?

_____

_____

_____

2. At that time, what did you think lawyers did? What was it about being a lawyer that you found attractive?

_____

_____

_____

3. Have you ever thought you should become a lawyer to make someone else happy? Who?

_____

_____

_____

4. Why does that person want you to become a lawyer? Are those reasons important to you? Why or why not?

_____

_____

5. Have your reasons for wanting to become a lawyer changed over time? If so, describe why you think you want to become a lawyer now.

_____

_____

_____

Coming Attractions

Considering a future career can be a bit like watching a preview for an upcoming movie. You don't see any of the boring parts. Based only on the highlights, it looks great. But before you buy a ticket, you usually read some reviews or ask your friends if it's any good, right? If you rely only on previews, you can end up wasting good money on a bad film. What's true for movies is also true for your career—only your career can last thirty or forty years and is a lot harder to walk out on if you don't like it.

The best parts of practicing law can be exciting indeed. Winning a trial. Closing a deal worth millions. Helping a needy family avoid eviction. Drafting legislation. Negotiating a contract for an entertainment superstar. Winning government approval for a new medication. Convicting a criminal. Assisting in the adoption of a child. Counseling a couple about their wills. Structuring a company's finances to save it from angry creditors.

Maria Mangano of Durham, North Carolina, experienced the thrill of overcoming adversity to achieve a good outcome through the legal system. "It was late in the day and I was getting ready to leave when the call came in. A kid had gotten kicked out of the High School of Science and Math, a very competitive public school that you had to apply to get into. He was expelled for what appeared to be a trivial offense, without any due process whatsoever," she recalls. "We had to go in for a TRO [temporary restraining order]. We had to get the court to order him back to school immediately, or he'd never catch up. A trial in a couple of years would do him no good at all." The time pressure made the case more difficult. "It was a little law office. Just me and one other lawyer. We had to work hard and work fast—we wanted to be in court the next day. When we went to prepare the complaint, the computer and printer went on the blink. We actually had to file pleadings printed on a dot matrix printer.

"We really felt this kid had been wronged. His rights had not been respected in the slightest. And we won an injunction. We got him back in school the next day. It was one of those truly satisfying moments in the law. I really cared about helping this person and creating principles of law that would help other students. It was my most thrilling moment as a lawyer. We got covered in the paper. It was one of the few times I was happy being adversarial."

Every thrilling legal performance requires a great deal of preparation and practice. Usually that preparation is far from exciting. (That's legalese for "deathly dull.") What's more, the highlights in a legal career may be few and far between. Especially for lawyers with less experience, who often have to turn things over to more senior lawyers to handle the fun stuff.

Imagine. You've just graduated from a top-ten law school and you've landed a job in one of the best New York law firms. Plush offices. Tea carts rumble around every afternoon at three. You think you've made it.

Kent Frankstone thought he'd live happily ever after. But at the end of his first day on the job he got a hint that his dream might fade. As part of his orientation, he'd been shown the firm's two-floor law library, conference rooms replete with tasteful artwork and furniture, and numerous partners' window offices boasting views over Manhattan. His last stop on the tour was the Human Resources Office, where he was given travel expense forms. His tour guide smiled knowingly and said, "I think you'll get a lot of experience filling these out."

Before he knew it, Kent (a newlywed) was sent for months at a time to cities around the country, where he sat in windowless storage rooms reviewing stacks and stacks of documents in file folders and boxes. "I had to read each piece of paper and summarize its contents so that a partner could decide how important the document was." Kent's vantage point affected his view of the job. "I began to realize that on the intellectual food chain, I was at the bottom. It would take me a long, long time to fight my way up to the top."

In order to think objectively about law, you have to look at both sides. Good and bad. I'll discuss more about each later. It's still your turn to do some soul searching.

1. The five reasons I most want to become a lawyer are: _____

_____

_____

_____

2. The five most serious doubts I have about becoming a lawyer are:

_____

_____

_____

3. The three skills that will help me become a good lawyer are: _____

_____

_____

_____

4. The three weaknesses that could keep me from becoming a good law-

yer are: _____

_____

_____

_____

5. The three things that I expect to find most satisfying about the practice

of law are: _____

_____

_____

_____

6. The three things that I expect to find least satisfying about the practice

of law are: _____

_____

_____

_____

The Vision Thing

Becoming a lawyer is not an end in itself. It's a beginning. Or a means to an end. For some, law is a means to change the world. Feed the hungry. House the homeless. Defend the defenseless. Bring equality into the everyday life of those denied it.

A woman I'll call Susan saw law as a way she could address what she describes as rampant injustice against Hispanics in the United States. "I wanted to go to law school to have power and to help my people. In this country, it's important to know your rights." Susan works as a public defender in a large eastern city, where her fluency in Spanish and her dedication to a cause has helped her provide more personal and supportive legal advice to many who are literally misunderstood by the criminal justice system.

For others, law represents the system. To get ahead, you have to understand the system. Maybe you can't beat the system, but at least the system won't beat you. Marty Woelfle, who now prosecutes environmental crimes for the U.S. Department of Justice, had her ideas about what a lawyer does shaped both by television and by personal experience. Television shows like *Perry Mason* and *The Young Lawyers* showed lawyers in positions of power. "If you wanted authority and independence, law was one of the few fields you could go into. Also, my mom was divorced when I was young. I saw how hard she struggled and how she had to do what others told her. So I sought security and autonomy in law."

And for some, law is a means to a lifestyle. Money. Prestige. Power. Becoming a lawyer can represent a form of success. Elaine Johnston comes from a family with few college graduates in it. "The attraction of law for me was having the professional credential—a credential that I couldn't have otherwise." Maria Mangano had gotten her master's in English and was poised to get her Ph.D., but was talked out of it by her parents. "My parents are children of immigrants. They think the best thing anyone can do is to get an education and enter one of the professions."

For still others, the desire to go to law school doesn't necessarily reflect a desire to become a lawyer. "I have a completely upside-down view of the reasons for going to law school," says Christopher Goelz of Mercer Island, Washington. "Most people have an end in mind: they want to become lawyers. And they suffer through three years of law school to reach that end. But just going to law school is a great thing. You get to think about interesting issues and discuss them with interesting people. The downside is that you become a lawyer. The vast majority of people I know who are lawyers are not all that satisfied with their professional lives. If you want to go to law school, go to law school. Then figure out what you want to be. It's really perplexing to me that so many people see law school as a means to an end and it's hard to see why that end should be such a powerful draw given how most people feel about it when they get there."

What is it that you think getting a law degree will help you do?

1. A law degree will help me achieve the following life goals: _____

_____

_____

2. When I retire, I want to be remembered for the following accomplish-

ments: _____

_____

_____

_____

3. Unless I go to law school, I will not be able to: _____

_____

_____

_____

Dear Diary

Go back over what you've written so far. Keep your answers in mind as you continue through this book. At the end of the book, return to this chapter. Repeat these questions and compare your latest answers with your initial answers. As with reading a diary you kept as a kid, you may learn something from what changes and what stays the same.

▪ 3 ▪

LEGAL MYTHOLOGY

Santa Claus delivers presents to good children every year on Christmas Eve. Smoking is sexy. We can reduce the federal budget deficit, increase military spending, and lower taxes.

Remember how you felt when you discovered that something you really wanted to believe was just a myth? Well, it's that time again. Many popular perceptions about the law are nothing more than myths. They may have been true once upon a time. Long ago, in simpler days. But now they are just a modern form of fairy tale.

Reality Bites

We're going to take a look at some of the most popular myths about life after law school. Add a couple of your own, and we'll have the top ten wrong reasons to go to law school.

Legal Myth No. 1: *Law is safe.* I haven't seen the answers you wrote to the questions raised in the previous chapter. Still, I bet a lot of you said you thought about going into law for the security. Even if you didn't put that down, you probably thought about it. We've all thought or heard this. The professions are safe. Become a doctor or a lawyer and you've got it made.

At first blush, it makes sense. People will always need lawyers. Every year, at every level of government, lawmakers are making laws. Someone has to help the public interpret them. Comply with them. Evade them. So every law increases the need for lawyers. And some laws *really* increase the need for lawyers. It seems that nearly every year some major piece of legislation is described (by lawyers themselves) as a full-employment-for-lawyers act. Until legislators stop judging their success by the number of acts enacted, there will be plenty of laws for lawyers to deal with.

What's more, we're the litigation society, right? Everybody is suing everybody else over everything. Remember the guy who used his lawn mower as a hedge clipper? When he got hurt lifting the mower (blade spinning) over the bushes to cut them, he sued the company that made the mower. Won a big jury verdict too. You don't think that just anybody could dream up a theory to justify paying that man money, do you? No. It took a lawyer to do that. And don't forget that it also took a lawyer to defend the company that lost the case because it failed to warn people not to use the lawn mower to cut bushes. As theories for emptying deep pockets have multiplied, so too has the need for lawyers to litigate both sides of an expanding number of controversies.

Why, then, is it a myth to say that law is safe? Simply because there are too many lawyers chasing too few jobs. Don't get me wrong. I'm not joining the lawyer bashers out there. I won't blame all the ills of our society on the fact that the United States is overlawyered. I'm just making a simple economic argument. Supply and demand.

Each year more than 40,000 new lawyers graduate from law school and flood prospective employers with their résumés. Jobs are not waiting for a significant percentage of these law grads. The National Association of Law Placement reports that only about 70 percent of the class of 1993 had found full-time employment in a "law-related position" six months after graduating from law school. Fully 13 percent remained unemployed, while 16.7 percent either had found part-time or nonlegal positions or had stopped looking for work. Increasingly, recent law school grads find they must work as paralegals or with a "temporary lawyer" agency before landing their first full-time position. A March 1995 article in the *ABA Journal* cites this trend as especially strong on the East and West Coasts, where work is more difficult to find.

Law schools try not to talk too much about it, but not all of their graduates can find jobs. Sure, if you can get into a top-ten law school, you're not likely to have a problem. But at other schools many students are struggling with a tight job market. One law school Dean of Admissions described the current situation as a "moral dilemma" for law schools. "To keep our numbers of applicants up, we paint a rosy picture of the advantages of coming to law school. What we're not telling those prospective students is that if you're not in the top thirty percent of the class, you're going to have a hard time finding a law-related job."

It's no fun to be a third-year law student or a recent law grad without a job offer in hand. One lawyer recalls how hard it was to break into the profession. "After law school, I had to work for a judge as a legal bailiff on the criminal calendar and part-time at a Mexican restaurant to pay the bills. Through the bailiff position, I got to know a lot of public defenders and prosecutors. After a couple months as a bailiff, I applied and got a job at the County Attorney's office making $21,000 a year."

Once you find a legal job, you are still not safe. The corporate management trend of the 1990s is employee layoffs. Don't think that corporate legal departments are immune. Law departments do not contribute directly to a corporation's bottom line, so it is easy to question their value when times are tough. A legal "product" is much harder to see and to value. So lawyers are among those joining the unemployment lines. One major accounting firm recently fired more than half the sixty-five attorneys in its corporate legal department along with two hundred support staff.

Law firms are not havens from these pressures. Legal magazines and newspapers routinely report on associate layoffs at large firms. Associates get fired at medium and small firms too; it just doesn't make the news. One lawyer at a twenty-lawyer firm told what happened to the entering class of three lawyers. "The firm hired the three of us in the fall and fired the other two lawyers by Christmas. They really only wanted one lawyer, but hired three and tried us out for three months. That way they could keep whoever was best." Most of the lawyers who join firms nationwide never become partners. This is especially true at large firms in big cities. Few private firms know what to do with lawyers who don't make partner. So it's up or out.

Even making partner is no longer a guarantee of lifetime tenure. More and more firms are "firing" partners who fail to maintain an active practice. Bring in the business or make room for someone who will. A private survey of 105 large firms conducted by Hildebrandt, Inc., and summarized in the *ABA Journal* indicates that 59 percent of those firms had terminated partners in the preceding eighteen months.

Whole firms can implode. During the 1980s, Finley, Kumble, Wagner, Heine, Underberg, Manley, Myerson & Casey grew at an astonishing pace to become one of the nation's largest firms. Then it simply disintegrated. When firms like Finley Kumble or New York's venerable Lord, Day & Lord disband, there are scores, or even hundreds, of lawyers dumped on the job market at one time. (I had offers to work at both those firms—even spent one of my law school summers at Lord Day—and often wonder how things would have been different for me had I joined either of them.) The bottom line: For several years now, the market for lawyers has been a "seller's" market, and you're a potential "buyer."

Legal Myth No. 2: *I'll get rich.* As one lawyer put it, "You have a greater chance of being an NFL football player than you do of being a wealthy law partner." You can definitely make a decent living as a lawyer, but you are very unlikely to amass a fortune. My law school classmates who are really well off today didn't get that way by practicing law. They became investment bankers, inherited money, or married well. If your goal in thinking about the law is to make money, you should try one of those options instead. Or write a great thriller, like lawyers Scott Turow and John Grisham. Or buy lottery tickets.

There are good reasons why lawyers—especially newer lawyers—do less well than popularly thought. First, legal education is frightfully expensive. Tuition at private university law schools can approach $20,000 per year for tuition and room and board. After three years of that kind of punishment, you could be starting out with a student loan balance in the high five figures. (Congratulations. A new law lets you pay off your law school loans over thirty years, so you can think about alma mater at least once a month for a long time.) Those loans may require you to accept the "golden handcuffs" of a well-paying, but less than satisfying, position. But even if you land one of the better-paying jobs, you may not be able to get rid of the old Honda just yet.

Second, in your early years as a lawyer you are subsidizing those who graduated before you. Whether you end up in private practice, in a corporation, or as a GS 9 in the government, you'll be at the bottom of a pyramid. Some form of seniority system will restrain your upward mobility. You're likely to face years of lockstep salary adjustments before you break into partnership or become a vice president. And even then the money may be good but not great, unless you make it to the very top of a big corporation's legal department or become a partner at a big-city law firm.

A 1994 Supplement to *The National Law Journal* provides a good overview of what many different lawyers around the country are paid. For example, among in-house attorneys, median total compensation for entry-level attorneys was $58,000 (remember that many entry-level corporate counsel have years of experience elsewhere), for section heads was $110,000, and for general counsel was $127,530. In general, salaries were lower in the South and West, and higher in the Northeast. Large firms pay their starting associates well. Expect about $44,000 in Louisville, $52,000 in Seattle or Denver, $70,000 in Los Angeles, and $83,000 in New York. Associate salaries are kept high at least in part to compensate top law school grads for taking the great risk that they will never become partners of the firm.

Third, most lawyers do not reap the money of big-firm lawyers—or even the money of other jobs that don't have the same popular perception of being well-paying. The March 1995 issue of *Money* magazine ranked America's "50 Hottest Jobs." *Money* pegged the median annual earnings of lawyers, after ten years' experience, at $58,500. Certainly not a shoddy number, but less than other positions, including some that require less expensive and time-consuming education. Jobs with higher median annual salaries than law include: physician/surgeon ($156,000/$200,000), airline pilot ($95,794), stockbroker ($90,000), college sports instructor and coach ($75,000), computer engineer ($70,000), food service and lodging owner ($62,000), management consultant ($60,000), and commercial property manager ($60,000). Following close behind lawyers are construction managers ($55,999), religious directors ($54,350), physician assistant ($53,225), and computer systems analyst ($53,000).

Today's very top lawyers are indeed paid quite well. But the very top lawyers have been out of law school for a long time—and they got out of law school when there were far fewer lawyers crowding the market. According to *The National Law Journal*, the average 1993 graduate from the University of Maine, Dickinson, Case Western Reserve University, and the University of Alabama law schools took jobs with a starting salary in the range of $32,000 to $36,000. That isn't significantly more than the $31,722 paid to starting public school teachers in my hometown. And the lawyers certainly don't get the summer off.

Legal Myth No. 3: *I'll be my own boss.* One aspect of the American Dream is to control your own destiny. Law may seem like one of the last ways for those not independently wealthy to capture that dream. But as a lawyer, you are very unlikely to find the freedom to be your own boss. You won't control your own destiny if you join the legal department of a corporation. Or if you join a big law firm—at least not until you become top dog there. Or if you become a government lawyer. There are constant constraints in the form of cost-conscious clients, billable-hours targets, difficult partners, internal and external politics, and the simple press of time. These constraints restrict the freedom you will have to do the kind of work you want, when you want, and with whom you want.

You may find independence at work through handling "your own" matters. But by definition, each of your clients is your boss even if no one you work with is. Like it or not, law is a service business. You have to provide service to your client when your client wants it, not when you want to provide it. I have to remind my wife of this every time a client calls late at night, or on Thanksgiving Day, or while we're on vacation. You cannot serve your clients well if you're only willing to serve them when it suits your schedule. Whether you become a solo practitioner with no one to report to or a government lawyer with superiors throughout the bureaucracy, you will have at least as many bosses as you have clients.

Legal Myth No. 4: *I'll try cases.* Perry Mason. F. Lee Bailey. Gerry Spence. Marcia Clark. Racehorse Haynes. The popular perception of lawyers is the bright, tireless, always successful trial lawyer. Exposing lies on cross-examination. Righting wrongs. Living in the courtroom.

Not surprisingly, many students thinking about becoming lawyers picture themselves trying case after case. Becoming the heroes they read about in books or watched on TV. Winning millions for grieving widows or convicting vicious criminals.

You might, you just might, get to live out this dream. But the odds are against it. Let's assume that you were hired by someone or you started your own practice with the idea that you would handle litigation. You cleared the first major hurdle.

"So, when do I get to try my first case?"

"Slow down. You're just out of law school. You need training. Depositions. Arguments to the court about motions. Besides, Tom over there has been waiting three years for his first trial, so he's in line ahead of you. And all the cases you're working on right now will probably settle before trial."

The realities of trial practice will likely keep you from trying many cases, especially early in your career. Many clients cannot tolerate the expense and risk of taking a case all the way to trial. Why would a rational client pay the high costs of preparing a case for trial if there was any significant risk of losing? It usually makes good sense to compromise. Settle for an amount of money that is not ideal, but that is risk-free.

Settlements also avoid the wait for a day in court. American courts are so backlogged that it is simply impossible for them to try even 10 percent of the cases now pending. The federal judges in Connecticut, for example, each recently had an average of over 650 cases assigned to them. Even if people stopped filing new cases, it would take years and years to try all those cases. Since that will never happen, settlements are essential. Nationwide, 95 percent of all cases (civil and criminal) settle. Mostly because the courts demand it. They would simply grind to a halt otherwise.

Even if you prepare a case that's among the 5 percent of civil cases that will make it to trial, there's probably a more senior lawyer still waiting for the chance to get some trial experience who will grab it. Or, having spent all that money to prepare for trial, the client may demand that a seasoned trial lawyer present the case. One associate with a large law firm told me this story: "I was handling an employment discrimination case for a big client of the firm. I handled all the discovery. Did all the depositions. Wrote all the briefs. Even prepared all the witnesses for trial. But when the case was called, the client said a partner had to try it. They got scared that an associate would blow the case. It really burned me, but you can understand it from the client's point of view." As a new lawyer, you may face a classic catch-22: you won't be given trial experience until you become an experienced trial lawyer.

Some plaintiff's lawyers, insurance defense lawyers, and prosecutors still try a lot of cases. You can increase your chances of fulfilling a dream of trying cases by working in one of these positions. Otherwise, like most "trial lawyers," you may end up as a "litigator," handling the paperwork and preparations for trial but rarely examining witnesses in open court.

Legal Myth No. 5: *Law is glamorous.* When I think of a glamorous career, I think of acting. Performing in public. Lots of publicity. The limousines, the elegant evening wear, the big money. All of that must sound silly and unrealistic to the New York waitress trying to break into Broadway and to the Beverly Hills car wash employee hoping for a screen test.

Well, describing law as glamorous sounds downright silly to most lawyers, slogging away in the legal trenches. Sorry to burst your bubble, but answering interrogatories and reading documents by the truckload is *not* glamorous. Preparing public utility rate increase requests is *not* glamorous. Plea bargaining a drunk driving charge is *not* glamorous. Searching land records is *not* glamorous.

Lawyers work hard. Very hard. Often their work is tedious. Even when something that lawyers work on makes news—a huge corporate merger, a front-page lawsuit—it is usually the clients, not the lawyers, who are the focus of attention. Most lawyers working on those big deals or big lawsuits labor anonymously behind the scenes.

What's more, the stresses that practicing law puts on many lawyers have far from glamorous results. "Law has a tremendous impact on the balance in your life. I have real reservations whether a person can have a high-powered career in law *and* a happy marriage *and* happy kids— especially if his or her spouse also has a high-powered career. It can be done, but it's almost impossible to have a fulfilling family life with two high-powered careers," says Becky Henderson, a lawyer who has tried full-time and part-time practice in small and medium-size law firms in two states. "I don't think it's possible to be a good lawyer and leave work at five every day, to be a good lawyer and not work weekends, to be a good lawyer and not walk around with a high stress level about all the things you ought to be doing."

The competing demands of professional and family life eventually caused Becky to stop practicing. "There may be room somewhere in the profession for the outstanding woman lawyer with an outstanding family life, but I haven't found it. I do know many highly successful women lawyers who have no children or are not married—or are not happily married. Some women practice full-time and delegate all their child care, but that's not what I wanted to do," she continued. "Many women who have been outstanding lawyers and do a solid job at home get out of the practice by retiring altogether or by becoming magistrates or going into the government.

"The awful thing about this observation is that you can't explain it to someone else until they've done it themselves. I tried to explain my feelings to a woman on law review, who was filled with ambition. I could tell she thought that I simply wasn't as high-powered as she was, that she could make it work even though I hadn't. But sometime later I got a letter from her in which she said that everything I told her had been true."

The pressures that Becky describes for women lawyers are also felt by many men—as I can personally attest. In a profession where your productivity is measured by hours billed, the more productive you are at the office, the less time you can devote to being a good husband or father. The compromises that result from this kind of pressure can leave lawyers—men and women alike—feeling as if they are not successful in any aspect of their lives. Not a very glamorous feeling.

Legal Myth No. 6: *Law is a profession, not a business.* Law has historically attracted people who wanted a more genteel, less cutthroat career. The idea that lawyers treated each other courteously and presumed each other to be honorable was once deeply ingrained. When our parents were deciding on their careers, law really was a profession rather than a business. Lawyers were content merely with earning a comfortable living, clients forged long-term relationships with law firms, partners in law firms had tenure for life.

Times have changed. Some lawyers over fifty still cringe when they hear law described as a business, but that's the reality. Today there are legal p.r. firms, marketing consultants, advertising firms, business planners, and others out selling advice to law firms desperate to survive in a competitive marketplace. Law and business now share the same emphasis on the bottom line. Today, when the profitability of their organization falls, lawyers in both corporations and law firms are downsized, right-sized, and simply laid off. A lawyer who left a small San Francisco firm remembers: "The place was relatively progressive, but the importance of money to the process was troubling. Everybody was always out there trying to get money for themselves or someone else." One in-houser told me that, although she enjoyed what she was doing, she had no job security whatsoever. There is a constant threat of a "rif," a reduction in force, if the company's results are poor. "I could get fired for no reason. I could get riffed. It's just a fact of corporate life in the nineties."

There is a widespread perception today that lawyers have become money-grubbing. Lawyers will accept only cases that they think will be profitable. Lawyers pad their bills. In early 1995, *U.S. News & World Report* found that 69 percent of Americans believe "lawyers are only sometimes honest or not usually honest" and 56 percent feel "lawyers use the system to protect the powerful and enrich themselves." Lawyers hear these perceptions. One lawyer I talked to described meeting someone who, upon learning she was talking to a lawyer, promptly launched into a matter-of-fact speech about what a shame it was that all lawyers had to cheat their clients out of money. "I was so offended that this total stranger was essentially accusing me of being a thief, but that's what people think of lawyers today."

Maybe there is some truth in the popular perception. One lawyer I spoke to was clearly disillusioned. "In the firm there were unquestionably true gentlemen, who were outstanding lawyers and outstanding people. But it's rarer and rarer. It's harder and harder to make money practicing law, so the principled lawyers stand out among the fairly materialistic and aggressive lawyers out there who are trying to make more money than you can reasonably make practicing law. The new economics of practicing law puts pressure on people to overbill and to manufacture work. There is now a sort of desperate edge to the monetary aspect of law."

Hiring a lawyer or a law firm has become an economic decision. Private law firms no longer simply dictate the hourly rates that they will charge their clients. Instead, corporations are demanding that law firms share the risk of poor results through alternative billing arrangements. Clients perform audits of law firm activities and billings. Payment of legal bills is delayed, or compromised. Lawyers are being sued for malpractice in record numbers. And many more lawyers are being disbarred, suspended, or reprimanded by grievance committees each year than was the case only a few years ago.

The relationship of lawyers to their partners has changed. If a lawyer or group of lawyers can make more money elsewhere, they will split off on their own or join another firm. If a lawyer or group of lawyers—even partners—are seen as "deadwood," they may be asked to leave. That's just what *The National Law Journal* reported happened at Cadwalader, Wickersham & Taft in late 1994, when seventeen partners were "pushed out" of the firm.

Even the way lawyers deal with each other has become less civil. "I have felt uncomfortable since day one as a lawyer with the adversarial aspects of the profession," said one lawyer practicing with a firm in a southern city. "In my first week of practice we had some motion we wanted to file a little late, so I called up the other side to get their consent. The lawyer on the other side was someone I had gone to law school with, someone I had studied for the bar exam with. She said no. I couldn't believe it. There was no reason why her client would care whether we filed today or a month from today. Then it hit me. This is the adversarial system."

Many jurisdictions have enacted codes of conduct for lawyers. These codes themselves show the depths to which conduct by some lawyers has sunk. Here's an example of some of the rules that bar associations have felt compelled to put into writing:

- Civility and courtesy are the hallmarks of professionalism and should not be equated with weakness;
- I will not knowingly make statements of fact or of law that are untrue;
- I will refrain from utilizing litigation or any other course of conduct to harass the opposing party;
- I will refrain from engaging in excessive and abusive discovery, and I will comply with all reasonable discovery requests;
- In depositions and other proceedings, and in negotiations, I will conduct myself with dignity, avoid making groundless objections, and refrain from engaging in acts of rudeness or disrespect;
- I will not file frivolous motions. . . .

No, law isn't a haven of gentility anymore.

Legal Myth No. 7: *I'll save the world.* One of the most noble reasons to go to law school is to gain a license to do good for others. Lawyers do have great opportunity to help others and to perform good works. The environmental movement has depended heavily on lawyers. Advocates for the homeless, the handicapped, and those with AIDS are often lawyers. Desegregation of the public schools was brought about almost entirely by a small group of lawyers. Less well known is the fact that thousands of lawyers in corporations and law firms volunteer their time to assist the needy with their legal problems, such as landlord-tenant disputes, divorce and child custody issues, and employment matters.

The difficulty, once again, is a matter of numbers. Those saving the world, or a little piece of it, usually do so through nonprofit organizations, such as the Southern Poverty Law Center, the NAACP Legal Defense and Educational Fund, the Lawyers Committee for Human Rights, and the Sierra Club. These and similar groups often need lawyers, but can't often afford to pay many. There are more lawyers interested in working for them than there are positions to fill. So the competition for those few positions is intense. A big firm like Cravath, Swaine & Moore may hire forty new lawyers a year, and there are twenty-three firms as large as Cravath based in New York City alone. The NAACP Legal Defense and Educational Fund might hire one or two lawyers nationwide.

Martha Davis, an attorney with the NOW Legal Defense and Educational Fund, acknowledges that she was very fortunate to land her position. "The competition for these jobs is intense. The reason I got the job, I'm sure, is that I had done so much pro bono work while I was at Cleary, Gottlieb, Steen & Hamilton. It wasn't like I was just another lawyer who wanted out of a big firm. I had some practical experience to offer."

Sure, you can join a private law firm and still volunteer your time to help out a deserving organization, but the pressure on lawyers who spend too much time on pro bono work can be intense. Remember, law is a business. Few firms will permit you to sacrifice very many billable hours for nonbillable pursuits. The American Bar Association urges law firms to pledge that their lawyers will spend at least fifty hours a year on pro bono work. That number often becomes a ceiling rather than a floor. You will be able to save only a very small piece of the world in fifty or a hundred hours a year of volunteer time.

Truth and Justice

There is at least one negative myth about lawyers that I should also debunk. *Lawyers are selfish jerks.* Lawyers have become the favorite targets of late-night talk-show hosts. Lawyer jokes abound.

- Why don't sharks attack lawyers? Professional courtesy.
- Why does California have the most lawyers and New Jersey has the most toxic-waste dumps? New Jersey got first choice.
- What's the difference between a lawyer and a catfish? One is an ugly, scum-sucking, bottom-feeding scavenger, and the other is a fish.

The popular press has contributed to the lawyer bashing. Much has been written recently that is critical of lawyers. Some of that criticism is even deserved. But most of it focuses on the excesses of a very small percentage of lawyers.

Dan Read, a solo practitioner in Durham, North Carolina, made the point very nicely. "The satisfaction of helping people directly in their struggles to make a decent life for themselves and achieve such justice as they can, to help them discover and enforce their powers and rights, to advance the condition of the world we live in a little bit, these are all intensely satisfying, even amid what is often drudgery and difficulty. Naturally, the profession attracts, and receives, undue bad publicity because of unscrupulous, self-interested people—but overall I think highly of my colleagues and the work that they do. Many of the truly noble people I know are lawyers, and I am proud to be an attorney myself."

The typical lawyer contributes positively to our society and our economy. He or she really does help solve problems—often by thinking ahead and devising ways to avoid them. When properly focused, the intelligence, care, and savvy of lawyers help many in our society—corporations and individuals alike—avoid and resolve difficulties of all kinds. Even to find justice.

The Beatings Will Continue Until Morale Improves

Congratulations. You're all the way through the bad news, and you're still reading. Either you're facing a quiz on this chapter in your pre-law class or you have more than a passing interest in the law.

I deliberately gave you the bad news first. It weeds out the fainthearted more quickly, plus it makes the good news (next chapter) sound that much better.

Before we leave the subject of bad news, though, we should do a little self-reflection.

1. Of all the things I read about legal myths, the most disturbing to me was:

_____

_____

_____

2. I intend to do further research or talk to others who might be able to help me avoid the following concern:

_____

_____

_____

3. I now realize that I probably would not be happy in a job in which I had to:

_____

_____

_____

4. Another reason not to go to law school is:

_____

_____

_____

Good. Now tuck those answers and all your doubts about law practice away. You'll want to return to them later.

· 4 ·

REAL LAWYERS

Ready for some good news? Okay. The practice of law can be really fun. Challenging. Interesting. Even exciting.

You want to decide that for yourself? Sure. Let's take a specific example. Just yesterday I got some news about one of my cases. The judge had decided an important motion for preliminary injunction in favor of our client. Yes! Make my day!

What's so thrilling about getting a good decision? The decision came in a hotly contested case. Two large pharmaceutical companies were each claiming the other had made false claims about the companies' competing prescription drugs. Millions and millions of dollars were at stake. Preparation for the preliminary injunction hearing (a short trial early in the case) had been intense: reviewing and analyzing thousands of documents, taking depositions of many witnesses, meeting with experts, learning complex medical information, writing briefs on many factual and legal issues, and, of course, conducting the actual hearing. It felt great to know that a lot of hard work had paid off. Our "team" couldn't have been happier.

But the result wasn't the only good thing about that case. During preparation and trial, I worked with a group of bright, interesting people. Several lawyers from Washington, D.C.'s Wilmer, Cutler & Pickering, including Tom Olson and Susan Crawford, a pair of savvy, hardworking litigators. K. S. Reagan, a lawyer with a small Washington firm that specializes in Food and Drug Administration issues. Lawyers, marketing and sales people, research specialists, and others employed by my client. And highly qualified professionals hired just for this case, including a medical school professor/cardiologist, an expert on consumer perception surveys, and a pharmacist/lawyer expert on pharmacy law issues.

Through that case I learned a lot about the pharmaceutical industry, sales of prescription drugs, federal and state regulation of prescription drug sales and advertising, and some fairly complicated medical issues.

37

These were subjects that I had never known much about before, and I found them especially interesting during this time of health-care debate. The lawyers on both sides received a quick, focused education that was an essential prerequisite to handling the lawsuit.

Working on that case was satisfying personally (I met some very interesting people), intellectually (I sure learned a lot), and professionally (there's nothing quite like working on a team that gets the job done). The case provided many challenges. We had to learn and analyze a large amount of complex information in a short period of time. We had to fit the facts as we knew them into our understanding of the law. Then we had to figure out how to package and present that information to the judge. After all, a large team had spent a few months educating themselves about the facts and the applicable law, but each side in the case had only a day and a half of testimony to explain its position to the judge.

That lawsuit highlights some of the things that I like most about practicing law. First, lawyers often enjoy variety in the issues they deal with at work. (I have worked on cases involving employment contracts, medical malpractice, insurance, soft contact lens patents, freedom of speech, police discipline, automobile accidents, design of aircraft engines, the purchase of a publishing business, activities of stockbrokers, and so on.) Whether a lawyer works in the context of lawsuits, financing agreements, regulatory compliance, or tax counseling, he or she will likely come into contact with a variety of businesses and industries. Lawyers working "in-house" at a particular company often find variety in the types of work they do, from litigation management to tax planning. There is a lot to be said for a job that treats you to variety. It's easier to stay fresh and interested in your work if you are learning and doing something new every day.

Second, lawyers work with and for smart, interesting people. By definition, lawyers are well educated. All received a graduate degree at law school, which means they must have done well in college. What is more remarkable is how talented and diverse lawyers are. Unlike most other graduate fields, law schools accept students who have excelled in almost any discipline. Poets, chemists, linguists, historians, psychology majors, accounting majors, and business majors are all potential lawyers. Medical school has required prerequisite courses (who could forget chemistry and biology?), and graduate programs in, say, engineering or architecture require undergraduate degrees in those fields. But not law. Because every college student is potentially "majoring in law," lawyers come from a greater variety of backgrounds than do other professionals.

Law is increasingly a second career. As a result, many lawyers bring with them the perspective and expertise developed in a first career. A sizable percentage of my law school class had earned Ph.D.s in their prior lives. Many women go to law school after raising their children. Law often attracts those who work in industries that come in contact with lawyers, such as accountants, journalists, law enforcement officers, health-care professionals, and businesspeople. Many universities even offer a joint law-MBA program. Let's face it, you will spend *a lot* of time with the people at work. It's a big plus to spend that time around people who have interesting and diverse backgrounds, who can expose you to new ideas and interests.

Third, law is often challenging. Legal advice is expensive, so it is usually called for only when a client is facing a new, demanding situation. Very often, lawyers are asked to offer advice about what will happen in the future, based on the limited information known now. Will a contract be enforceable if it includes particular language? What is the best way to structure a financial transaction and still comply with the tax laws? How will a judge rule in a lawsuit involving a specific set of facts not seen in other court decisions? This type of work is intellectually challenging. In fact, the intellectual challenge is one thing some former lawyers miss after leaving the law. One put it this way: "Business tends to be a lot of hard work and salesmanship, which you also need in the law. But then there's the purely intellectual side of law—solitary thinking about law and facts. In business, I don't find the same intellectual satisfaction, not the same pure intellectual challenge you get practicing law. In law, there's a better chance of being judged on how good you are, plain and simple."

When answers are required quickly (and when aren't they?), this work can also be physically challenging, as lawyers skip meals and lose sleep to get the job done. Anyone who has trained for an athletic competition can appreciate the satisfaction that can come from the sacrifice that meeting such challenges often requires.

Finally, lawyers are often working at the forefront of important societal issues. Health care. Copyright protection of computer software programs. The death penalty. Crime and punishment, generally. NAFTA. Salaries for athletes. How to help the homeless. Corporate mergers. Lawyers are involved in almost every news story in today's newspaper. Lawyers have the opportunity to help shape the responses to these and many other issues. If you're in the right place at the right time, you can have a great deal of impact as a lawyer.

The Devil Is in the Details

Of course, all of these rosy generalizations are still just generalizations. Unless we consider some specifics, we're at risk of simply creating new myths about the law.

I can tell you absolutely nothing about your specific interests and abilities, but I can tell you this: one person's perk is another's punishment. If you have an ethical problem with the death penalty, you will not enjoy prosecuting even the most interesting and challenging murder cases. If you panic at the thought of speaking on your feet, trial work will not be fun. If you have small children at home, "challenging" may not be the word that best describes working all night to close that corporate loan before the end of the fiscal quarter. Spending a week working with a client in Newport Beach or Denver or Miami or Phoenix will hardly be a vacation for the newlywed from Chicago.

To find happiness in the law, you must match your abilities, interests, and circumstances with the right job. *You* have to be comfortable with the match. If you don't like what you do, it won't help much that others think you'd enjoy it.

There are so many different things you can do with a law degree, there must be a job that will fit you like a glove. The problem, of course, is how to go about identifying that perfect legal position.

The task of finding your legal fit is not as daunting as it may seem. You may have geographic preferences that limit the choices. You may have preferences for working in a corporation, in a private law firm, in government, or in another specific setting. Most important, think back to your answers to the questions posed in Chapter 2 about why you are attracted to law. Those answers should provide you with important insights that limit the range of positions in which you would be happy. If you were attracted to law because of a desire to contribute to the solution of a societal problem, you should think about nonprofits and the government. If you are driven by a desire to make money, think about private law firms in large cities. If the intellectual aspects of law attract you, think about teaching.

To make the right choice, you can't lose sight of your objectives, your interests, and your abilities. Elaine Johnston spent several years at a private law firm before becoming assistant general counsel of the Smithsonian Institution, where she's much happier. "In private practice, I had no control over what I did. There was something of a hired-gun mentality. Now I feel like I've integrated my work with my personal interests. Work is no longer something I do just to make a living. What we're trying to accomplish at the Smithsonian is something I care about."

Learning a little more about jobs you think you might like is always a good idea, and that's where I can help. I am not going to try to describe all of the possible ways in which you could use a law degree. Instead, in this chapter, I will describe three general functions that lawyers perform, and will identify examples of positions in which lawyers typically perform those functions. The point here is to get you thinking about whether you have the skills and interests to fit into one of these three categories. We'll look at various legal jobs in more detail in Chapter 10.

All Law Is Divided into Three Parts

Let's look at what lawyers really do by grouping them into three broad (sometimes overlapping) categories based upon the lawyer's function. I call these three broad types of lawyers "advocates," "counselors," and "technicians." As you read these descriptions, think about which category best matches your interests and abilities.

Advocates

John Blume heads up the South Carolina Death Penalty Resource Center. "If a South Carolina inmate is indigent and sentenced to death, and their direct appeal has been denied, they're our responsibility. We represent them or find counsel for them." John began working with death penalty cases in the early 1980s and has been at the Resource Center since it opened in 1988.

"In this job, it's easy to become cynical. You see the justice system operating at its worst. Race and politics and other things that lots of people would have trouble believing do happen, like the police withholding evidence or prosecutors tampering with the jury pool. You see it over and over. So the work is very confrontational. There's no way to sugarcoat what we have to say—we're not arguing about somebody's money, we're arguing about somebody's life.

"And it's hard for me to imagine anything more at the core of what a lawyer should do. The decision to take a life is one of the most important decisions our legal system makes. It's also one of the most complex. And there are no set rules about how you make the decision. So when our system of justice is going to take someone's life, it's very important for skillful advocates to do all that they can to force the system to operate fairly."

Advocates like John Blume are lawyers who promote a position or seek to persuade. The trial lawyer is the obvious example, but submitting regulatory proposals to administrative bodies, lobbying legislators, and representing individuals in tax audits would also qualify. All lawyers to a greater or lesser extent advocate the position of their clients in some way—through the negotiation of a contract, the careful drafting of a will, or the communication of thoughtful business advice. The lawyers that I would classify as advocates, however, are only those whose *primary* job responsibility is to argue publicly on behalf of a client.

What type of person would enjoy being an advocate? Perhaps the most obvious trait shared by successful advocates is a strong sense of self-confidence. Another important trait of advocates is the ability to convince themselves that their client's position is the correct one. This is essential to good advocacy, because a jury or judge can quickly sense a lawyer's lack of belief in his client. Believing in your client is easy in many disputes where there is no obvious right or wrong answer—your view of who breached a contract or who started a fistfight depends largely on whose version of events you want to believe. But what about when a lawyer is asked to defend someone accused of a terrible crime? Or when a lawyer who cares strongly about the environment is asked to represent a polluter? The advocate must be able to resolve any conflict between personal beliefs and the client's position—or risk either personal dissatisfaction or professional ineffectiveness.

We have all heard criminal lawyers asked, "How can you represent that horrible guy?" A typical response is that everyone deserves a defense. True enough. Our system demands that each side of a controversy advocate its viewpoint strongly, with the hope that justice will emerge from that clash of positions. The advocate must agree with the assumptions underlying this system, for the advocate will be expected to take positions and make arguments that promote the client's interests, not those that represent what the lawyer personally believes is the "right" or "just" outcome.

"I'm part of Bill Clinton's generation, the 1960s and 1970s. If you're part of that generation and didn't burn your draft card or drop acid, you wanted to accomplish change through the system. Being a lawyer lets you accomplish that change," says Barrie Goldstein. She went into government work through the Justice Department's Honors Program, where she handled a variety of civil litigation. While at the Justice Department, her section was assigned to defend the Department of Housing and Urban Development against charges of racial discrimination. "I had entered the Justice Department thinking that I would be doing the noble thing, and here I was wearing the black hat. I thought about quitting, but my mentor said, 'Hey, learn to be a lawyer.' "

Advocates must have the ability to communicate well with all types of people. Good storytellers make great advocates because they can express ideas in a way that is interesting and effective. The ability to simplify the complex is also critical to the success of advocates. They must be able to take huge amounts of complicated or conflicting information, analyze it against legal standards, distill it to its essence, and communicate it to a decision maker in a persuasive fashion.

Would you enjoy the work of an advocate? If so, you should consider some of these positions: prosecutor, criminal defense lawyer, plaintiff's personal injury lawyer, insurance defense lawyer, divorce lawyer, and labor lawyer.

Counselors

Colleen Connor is an environmental lawyer who has advised clients both as an in-house counsel for a large corporation and as an attorney with a law firm. "When I was in private practice, I got a call from a client only one day before they had a meeting to respond to a complaint that they had exceeded the limits on a waste water discharge permit. They casually told me they had no defenses and said they were thinking about throwing themselves on the mercy of the New Jersey Department of Environmental Protection. I said that maybe we should talk things over.

"The client was several hours away, so I drove down there first thing in the morning. I spent several hours interviewing employees, while keeping one eye on the clock so that we wouldn't miss the meeting. When I learned more of the facts, it turned out that they *did* have good defenses to the complaint. The client simply didn't know the law well enough to recognize them. As things turned out, they were able to make a meaningful response and ended up paying a fine that was only a fraction of what the Department initially sought."

Counselors like Colleen Connor are primarily advisers. Once again, every lawyer is in some sense a counselor. But most of the lawyers that I would call counselors never get into court. Instead, counselors work in private consultation with their clients, guiding their personal and business decisions in a way that is intended to keep the clients out of legal difficulty or to gain some legal advantage.

Counselors range from the very specialized tax adviser to the general business adviser. What distinguishes a counselor is a thorough knowledge of a particular area of the law or a particular industry and the ability to apply that knowledge to solve problems. The "trusts and estates" lawyer who drafts wills is an expert in the laws governing the taxation and distribution of property after death. This type of counselor spends a great deal of time asking questions of and listening to his or her clients in order to understand their wishes. Only after doing so can the lawyer advise or counsel the client how best to achieve those wishes. The ultimate decisions remain the client's, but the counselor helps in the decision-making process by recommending how best to achieve those wishes within the constraints of the law.

Good counselors are good listeners. They seek to stimulate their clients to consider opportunities and problems that might otherwise have been overlooked—usually by asking probing questions. Counselors are also perceptive. They can distinguish between what a client says and what a client really means. Counselors bring their broad knowledge of law, business, and human relations generally to bear on a client's problem. They understand a client's business and can offer an objective evaluation of that business. In short, counselors are valued for their judgment. Judgment born of knowledge, experience, and careful thought.

If your skills and interests match those of a counselor, you should consider some of the following positions: in-house counsel, real estate lawyer, trademark and copyright lawyer, lending counsel, and employment lawyer.

Technicians

Becky Henderson worked for a fifteen-lawyer firm in Charleston, South Carolina, for about a year before the birth of her first child. She had passed the Virginia bar, but moved to South Carolina when her physician husband accepted a fellowship there. Because she was not yet admitted to practice in the state, Becky wasn't permitted to undertake certain tasks for the firm's clients. Instead, she did lots of the research to support other lawyers in the office. "I wrote something like six file-drawer-sized boxes of legal memos during that time," she said. "Each one was a quality product, the kind of work you'd hand in as a major paper in school. It was an extremely busy job in which I constantly had to prioritize my assignments and work things out among the partners. But I was still basically working as a law clerk. I'd write the brief and hand it off to someone else who would take it to court."

The things Becky was doing during that year placed her within the third category of lawyers, the technicians. Lawyers who implement legal advice by working, often behind the scenes, with little exposure either to the courtroom or to clients. It is commonly said that there are three types of relationships that lawyers within law firms have with clients: they are either "finders," "minders," or "grinders." Technicians are the grinders. The dedicated technicians don't get the glory that other lawyers may, but no law firm, corporation, or other legal service provider could survive without them.

Don't think that technicians are somehow less important lawyers than advocates or counselors. Technicians are essential to solving any complicated legal problem. Although the advocate may stand up and examine the witness in court, it is often a team of technicians who found the document used to cross-examine that witness.

I don't mean to imply that technicians never get into court or have client contact. Sometimes they do both—but on lower-profile or repetitive types of matters. Some corporations and law firms have lawyers who crank out the same type of legal product over and over: trademark applications, residential real estate contracts, securities law filings, lawsuits for the collection of small amounts of money. These activities often do not require the attention of an advocate or counselor. But they are still essential to the client and generate solid fees for the law firm.

Sometimes technicians are newer lawyers who have not yet blossomed into advocates or counselors. Other times, technicians are lawyers who have discovered that they are most productive when working on matters that require significant research, document review, and drafting. You would enjoy the role of a worker bee if you show attention to detail, have a good deal of patience, and do not need to see your name in lights.

Swarms of technicians can be found working on such matters as public stock offerings, class-action litigation, products liability (such as breast implant or asbestos exposure) cases, and large-scale pension or securities fraud litigation.

There are many challenging and stimulating legal jobs filled by advocates, counselors, and technicians. But a natural advocate would find working as a counselor or technician stifling. On the other hand, a technician might find being an advocate or counselor frightening. And someone who is not well suited to becoming a lawyer will not find any of these types of positions fulfilling. You've simply got to find the right fit.

· 5 ·

LEGAL SKILLS
AND INTERESTS

You *can* become a lawyer. Almost anyone can. That's the great attraction—and the great risk—of a career in law. In fact, choosing a career in law may be easier than choosing another career that's a better fit for you. For that reason, the most important question this book can help you answer is whether or not you *should* become a lawyer. In this chapter, I'm going to give you some "tips and tests" designed to help you see if you'll be happy as a lawyer.

The Perfect Job Description

In a famous First Amendment decision, U.S. Supreme Court Justice Potter Stewart said he wouldn't attempt to define pornography, "but I know it when I see it." A lot of us take the same approach to finding the right job. We can't really say what we want, but figure that we'll know it when we find it. Sadly, that approach often doesn't work.

Let's at least *try* to define what it is that you want in a job. Start by answering the following general questions.

1. My perfect job would involve the following day-to-day tasks: _____

_____

_____

2. I want to achieve the following balance between my work and personal lives: _____

_____

_____

3. When I think of a person I admire in the working world, the things I find most enticing about that person's job are _____

_____

_____

4. I want a job that makes me feel _____

_____

5. I want a job that gives me the freedom to _____

_____

_____

6. Right now, I think that the three most important reasons to work are

_____

_____

7. I want to work with people who _____

_____

_____

8. I want my work hours to be _____

_____

_____

9. In my job, I want to learn _____

_____

_____

10. My ideal job would be located in _____

_____

_____

Now go back over your answers and use them to write a single par-
agraph that describes your perfect job in general terms. Keep that par-
agraph handy as you read the descriptions in this book about what
different lawyers do and as you talk to people about their jobs. Compare
your "perfect job description" with what you discover others are doing.
Think about how closely your perfect job description matches what different lawyers actually do.

Each of us has personal interests and preferences that affect our enjoyment of work and working conditions. Let's try to figure out how your
interests and work preferences mesh with the practice of law. Read the
list of twenty statements below and circle the number that best indicates
how strongly you agree or disagree with each statement.

	STRONGLY AGREE		NEUTRAL		STRONGLY DISAGREE
1. I like thinking of ways to solve other people's problems.	5	4	3	2	1
2. I like brainteasers and/or crossword puzzles.	5	4	3	2	1
3. I like to read the newspaper and/or newsmagazines.	5	4	3	2	1
4. I enjoy research projects.	5	4	3	2	1
5. I like writing research papers.	5	4	3	2	1
6. I hate to speak in front of people I don't know.	5	4	3	2	1
7. I hate to give a speech to people I know.	5	4	3	2	1
8. I like the excitement of thinking on my feet.	5	4	3	2	1
9. I like history.	5	4	3	2	1
10. I don't like to argue unless my position is morally justified.	5	4	3	2	1

	STRONGLY AGREE		NEUTRAL		STRONGLY DISAGREE
11. I don't like to argue unless my position is logically correct.	5	4	3	2	1
12. I don't like to argue unless I think I can win.	5	4	3	2	1
13. I would rather argue about feelings than facts.	5	4	3	2	1
14. I do not like conflict.	5	4	3	2	1
15. I don't mind conflict, I just don't like it all the time.	5	4	3	2	1
16. I would rather influence a decision than be responsible for making it.	5	4	3	2	1
17. I like working with deadlines.	5	4	3	2	1
18. I would rather have too much to do than not enough to do.	5	4	3	2	1
19. I prefer to work on one task at a time, rather than many tasks simultaneously.	5	4	3	2	1
20. I don't like to admit that I don't know something.	5	4	3	2	1

This isn't the kind of test you can pass or fail. It should simply make you think about how your personal preferences may affect your enjoyment of law and what lawyers do. If your interests coincide with those who are happy in law, you should have circled a "4" or a "5" for Questions 1, 2, 3, 4, 5, 8, 9, 11, 17, and 18. You are also more likely to be happy as a lawyer if you circled a "1" or a "2" for Questions 6, 7, 10, 12, 13, 14, 15, 16, 19, and 20.

The following questions highlight some of the interests that should help you to be happy as a lawyer:

Desire to help others solve problems (Questions 1 and 16). Fundamentally, lawyers are paid to help people solve problems. This often requires becoming as fully involved with your clients and their problems as you would with members of your own family. To counsel your clients, you must know them and be well acquainted with their motivations.

In addition to providing legal advice, the best lawyers provide emotional and psychological support too when that is necessary. Charlotte

Morrissey recalls that her law firm represented the families of three airplane crash victims. "I was the primary associate on the cases. A trial would have been a severe emotional drain on the families and would not have taken place for several years. Besides, the only issue at the trial would have been how much money should be given to the families in compensation for the deaths. To avoid needless waiting and distress, we prepared 'demand' letters that included photographs, testimonials, examples of the victims' work, expert testimony on the victims' income-earning potential, and quotes from the family members describing the pain and suffering the deaths had caused. The letters, in essence, put a value on the lives lost in the crash and demanded just compensation for the loss.

"Gathering the information for the demand letters was a trying experience. I wanted to be certain that the families were compensated fairly, so I had to delve into emotional topics, review family photos, analyze the victims' school and work records, and speak to grieving employers, friends, and colleagues. Many, many conversations were interrupted by tears. Throughout the process, I felt I had to be steady as a rock—a support in time of need—someone who truly valued those who had died, and in a sense an avenging angel who would make sure that those at fault would pay for what had happened. It was very hard, but I felt like I was there for my clients when they needed me most."

Lawyers cannot be interested in solving problems only in the abstract; they should also enjoy becoming involved with people and should have a strong desire to help others. Some lawyers complain that "law would be great if it weren't for the clients." This refrain reflects an unhappiness or unease about becoming involved with the people behind the problems. Think about how you react when friends or family members bring their problems to you and you will gain an insight into how much you would enjoy becoming a lawyer.

Enjoyment of analysis (Questions 2–5 and 9). Lawyers investigate, organize, analyze, communicate, and predict. They must devise ways to understand recent history in order to predict future actions or events. The best lawyers undertake this analysis objectively, not emotionally. Do you enjoy painstaking investigation of facts, getting immersed in the details? Do you enjoy the reading, thinking, and organizing involved in preparing a long research paper? Do you enjoy writing that is factual and objective rather than creative or persuasive? The answers to these questions should help you decide whether you'd like doing what lawyers do.

Comfort with public speaking (Questions 6–8). Lawyers are sometimes put down as being mere "mouthpieces" for their clients. Setting aside the negative connotations of the description, that's exactly what lawyers do. They communicate for their clients. Lawyers speak to judges, juries, and most often to other lawyers. Whether on the phone or in person, one-on-one or to a large group, lawyers are always talking, often in "public." What's more, most "speeches" by lawyers are not made from prepared remarks, so lawyers have to be quick on their feet. Do you get shy or nervous talking to a group or to people you don't know? Do you feel uncomfortable speaking up in class or asking for directions? If so, there will be many times that you will feel uncomfortable as a lawyer.

Toughness in debate and negotiation (Questions 10–15). Much of what lawyers do involves debate and negotiation, argument and conflict. As a lawyer, your ultimate goal is to protect your client's interests. This means standing up to the bullies, staring down the stubborn, and convincing the hardheaded. Because lawyers deal with other lawyers, the guy on the other side thinks you're the stubborn bully—hence the conflict.

Some lawyers thrive on conflict and competition. As one Los Angeles lawyer put it, "I like the intellectual competitiveness of law. I like holing up in my office, plotting, strategizing, researching, writing, knowing that across town the 'enemy' is doing the same thing. In court, we unveil the results of all that solitary work and see who's done a better job, we see who WINS! I've always been competitive—sports mostly—and I like the winning and losing of law."

A good lawyer seeks to avoid conflict but is also tough enough to prevail when it arises. If you withdraw from conflict, you are unlikely to enjoy law. How do you react when someone cuts in front of you in a long line at the grocery store? Do you haggle over price when buying a car? Do you engage someone who expresses a political point of view with which you disagree? These experiences are clues to whether you would enjoy what lawyers do.

Reaction to pressure (Questions 17–19). Janet Nolan has faced the pressure of private practice as well as the pressure of representing the United States as an Assistant U.S. Attorney in New Jersey. "The stress is pretty amazing. You handle important cases and have many people counting on you and watching you. In private practice, it's partners, clients, and colleagues. In government work, the stress is in some ways less because your supervisors don't know as much about your cases as a partner in private practice would, but in some ways the pressure is greater because you have more responsibility."

As another lawyer put it: "In a firm, the fear of making mistakes is enormous, almost paralyzing. The attitude you have to adopt is that something you do wrong is not a mistake unless it can't be fixed. We 'practice' law to get it right. If you don't get it right the first time, you can usually fix it. Unless you look at things that way, you reach a point where you're scared to make any decision."

Lawyers deal in crisis. The phone rings and their priorities change: the client has an emergency, the trial will start next week, the deal has to close by the end of the month, we have to talk right away. Deadlines can be imposed by clients, colleagues, or courts. They are simply a fact of legal life, and they are constantly changing. With changing deadlines comes the juggling to accomplish everything you must when you must. Plans change, weekends are lost, vacations are canceled. The pressure can become intense. If you thrive on pressure and react well to deadlines, you are more likely to enjoy law. If you work best when you can control what you do and when, you may find the practice of law frustrating.

Acceptance of uncertainty (Question 20). Law is as much an art as it is a science. To some questions there is a right answer, but to most questions a lawyer can offer advice based only on judgment and experience. A lawyer must be able to admit that she doesn't know, for example, how a new statute will be interpreted, and yet still give advice in which her client will have confidence. If you are the type that needs to know there is a right answer and you have found it, you may find law difficult to practice.

What It Takes

Feelings of competence lead to feelings of happiness. You will be a happier lawyer if you feel competent at what you do. Based on my own observations and my interviews with lawyers, I have compiled an inventory of basic skills that you should have in order to practice law successfully. This list is by no means comprehensive, and it does not include the specific skills that relate to certain specialties in the law. (For example, a patent attorney who specializes in computer designs should certainly have some skill in engineering.) Still, if you do these things well, you have the raw ability to succeed in law.

1. *Reading.* A lawyer must be able to read detailed, complex documents and understand them. Often the reading is tedious and the writing poor. Nevertheless, the lawyer must be able to sift through the details and discern what is significant and what's not.

2. *Writing.* An attorney often has to communicate complex ideas and make them sound simple and logical. Style, grammar, and organization should help foster the communication, not distract from it.

3. *Speaking/Listening.* Attorneys spend a substantial amount of time

speaking to clients, the opposing attorney, witnesses, and representatives of the legal system. Just as with writing, a lawyer has to communicate clearly. A lawyer must articulate the client's position in a cogent, persuasive manner, no matter who the audience is. An attorney must also be able to engender trust when speaking, especially when dealing with clients, judges, or jurors.

The flip side of talking is listening. The most effective lawyers excel at listening. That means they pay attention to someone's words, tone, and body language to hear what's really being said. They follow up on offhand, but important, comments. And they filter through much of what they're told to get the information critical to the legal issues facing the client.

"Pay attention to what your client is saying or not saying. Be a student of human nature," advises one lawyer. "I think you have to realize that people are usually nervous when they meet with a lawyer and they tend to agree with everything. Then when they leave the office they forget important facts so you need to be sensitive about that. Try not to paraphrase and use too much jargon. Get your client to relax. Talk to them first."

4. *Prioritizing/Time Management.* Because most lawyers serve many clients, a lawyer must be able to manage time effectively and prioritize assignments. A procrastinator or a disorganized attorney will not fare well with clients or colleagues who are depending on them.

5. *Creativity.* Any lawyer can tell a client whether or not the client can undertake a proposed activity or resolve a dispute. The best lawyers find a way to make it happen that fits within the law.

6. *Ability to Work with Others.* Even if a lawyer is a solo practitioner, he or she will work with an administrative assistant, a paralegal, or other support personnel. A lawyer who practices with others will have to work well with colleagues.

7. *Analytical Skills.* All attorneys need to have the ability to reason. Analysis, the process of drawing logical conclusions from the facts, is a key component of any lawyer's job. Legal analysis is often by analogy. Lawyers have to apply the law to their client's situation before they can determine how best to advise their client. A primary tool for applying law to fact is the ability to compare one like situation to another.

8. *Conflict Management.* Conflict is a component of every lawyer's life. Some lawyers welcome conflict and thrive on it. Even those who do not enjoy conflict must learn how to manage it to the advantage of their clients.

9. *Ability to Learn.* Because of the complexity of law, no lawyer ever succeeds in mastering everything—that's why lawyers "practice" law. The most competent lawyers know how to teach themselves

quickly, either by relying on others to provide the necessary information or by collecting it themselves through research, interviews, or other information-gathering techniques.

10. *Dedication.* Law is hard work. It requires both a willingness to work long hours and a perseverance in the face of adversity and stress.

Do you possess some or all of these skills? If you are lacking some of these skills now, can you develop them in the future? If not, it may be time to begin thinking about whether the skills you do have could be better used in another career.

· 6 ·

LEGAL RESEARCH

You effort to decide whether or not to become a lawyer has gotten a solid start. You've examined your motives for thinking about law as a career, you've reviewed some of the popular myths about law and lawyers, you've heard advice from various lawyers around the country, and you've evaluated your legal interests and skills. Now you're ready to go out and become a lawyer, right? Maybe, maybe not.

Now it is time to act like a lawyer and conduct some "legal research" before reaching a definite conclusion.

Legal research can be a lot of fun. Kind of like solving a mystery. You know the answer to your question is out there somewhere. If only you look long and hard enough, you'll find it.

Just how hard and how long should you research a particular problem? When I was a law clerk, the answer was easy. I researched and researched until I was absolutely, positively certain that I had the right answer. When I joined a law firm, the decision about when to stop researching became harder. There was always a cost-benefit analysis to be done—was the value of the extra effort worth the marginal cost to the client?

You're now "researching" law as a possible career. How long should you work at investigating that issue? As long as it takes. You must do everything you can to get your career decision right the first time.

Let's look at what you should be doing to research law even after you finish this book.

Keep a Law Journal

You won't find the answer to the question whether law is the career for you in the library. As much as I hope this book has helped your thinking, you probably won't find the answer in this or in any other book. But you may find the answer in a journal, the journal you should be keeping to record your thoughts, interests, and goals about law as a career.

Your career journal provides a vehicle for you to continue the process you've started in this book. Continue the self-reflection and record your impressions. As you come into contact with lawyers, do further reading, or talk with career counselors, jot down notes about what you learn and how you react.

Some of you may find it helpful to have a section in your career journal where you keep a master list of pros and cons. As you think of things you'd like about a legal career, or that you'd dislike, add them to your list. Cross off pros or cons as your feelings change or as you learn more about law. Review the list every once in a while and chart how you feel over time. Are you becoming more or less enthusiastic as you learn more about law as a career? Why? Put that information into your journal too.

What's important is the trend. If you look back through your career journal and see a downward trend in your attitude toward law—especially as you learn more about it—alarm bells should go off. But you may miss the danger signs completely if you don't record your thoughts over a long period of time. So get writing.

Legal Resources

Where are you going to go digging for the information to help you make this decision? The best sources are practicing lawyers and people who got a law degree but aren't practicing.

I don't think I ever met a lawyer while growing up. None of my parents' friends were lawyers. There were no lawyers in my family. There was even some antilawyer sentiment. (My grandfather intentionally pronounces the word "lawyer" as "liar.")

Some of you will have a hard time finding lawyers to talk with about what they do. But some of you will have lots of lawyer contacts. Friends. Neighbors. Relatives. Friends of relatives. And so forth. Use these contacts. They are your legal resources, and you should mine them for nuggets of information.

If you don't know a lawyer and can't come up with someone who does, ask your college alumni or placement office for help. Many schools have lists of alumni who have volunteered to talk to prospective law students or to have them visit their office for a day or even for a week during the school's spring break. Look for other lawyers using school connections. Your local library (and certainly every law school and law firm library) will probably have a copy of a multivolume publication commonly called *Martindale-Hubbell*. This reference work lists hundreds of thousands of lawyers in private law firms. Look up the state, then the city where you are interested in working and start reading the short bios for the law firm lawyers listed there. When you come across someone who went to your college, call them up and ask to talk to them on the phone or to visit them for an informational interview. If you stress your school connection and the fact that you just want to get more information about the firm and the practice of law—that is, you're not asking for a job—you'll be more likely to get some of the lawyer's time.

Don't be shy about this. The worst that can happen is that the lawyer will turn you down. The best that can happen is that you will learn something useful about what another lawyer does—and perhaps make a contact that will be valuable to you in the future when looking for summer or permanent employment.

The best way to learn what a particular lawyer really does is to watch him or her in action. Try to spend a day or a week shadowing a lawyer at work. Sitting in the lawyer's office. What you see will be the real thing—provided you weren't brought along on a special, uncharacteristic day. After an ordinary day in my office, my ten-year-old daughter, Mariah, found the long conference calls I made "very boring." These conference calls with other lawyers were a part of my job that I would never have thought to describe to her. But by watching and listening to what I actually do, she got a more realistic picture than I could ever have given her.

Don't expect an exciting day. Following a lawyer around at work isn't exactly like going to the movies. But it's hard to imagine time better spent if you're serious about evaluating law as a career.

Another way to watch lawyers in action—and possibly to meet some lawyers in your area—is simply to drop by the nearest courthouse and sit in a courtroom during a trial. Trials are open to the public. No one will throw you out if you sit quietly in the gallery. And you're likely to see a little of what many lawyers consider the most fun they have at work. (Remember, for the vast majority of lawyers, examining witnesses in court is *not* what they do day to day. I'd bet that a majority of practicing lawyers have never seen the inside of a courtroom except when they were sworn in to the bar.)

Sitting in the back of the courtroom is a tried-and-true way to learn about trial lawyers. Former federal District Court Judge Robert C. Zampano got his start that way. "My family moved when I was in the sixth grade, but my parents didn't want me to change schools. So I took a bus each day that transferred in front of the courthouse. I had a ten- or fifteen-minute wait and sometimes I got cold, so I went into the courthouse to stay warm. Every day I'd sit in the courtroom and listen to cases. Pretty soon I started skipping buses when something interesting was happening. I used to meet all the lawyers. Sometimes they'd come over to me during breaks and say, 'Here's what I'm going to do, kid. Stick around.' The lawyers gave me all kinds of advice too. That's what got me going in the law." That start led him to become a U.S. Attorney in his early thirties and one of the youngest federal judges appointed to the bench.

Although you won't meet any lawyers, you can also see something of what happens in the courtroom by watching Court TV. Trials on Court TV may not be typical trials—certainly the O. J. Simpson trial is not a good example of the average criminal case. Still, Court TV is a lot more realistic than the weekly lawyer shows on television.

The only problem with shadowing a single lawyer or even sitting in on a trial is that you see only a tiny slice of the world of lawyers. Unless you are already sure that you want to be the type of lawyer you see in action, you may miss out on other opportunities for which you'd be better suited. So don't stop there. Track down every lawyer you can and talk to them. Each has a story to tell about how they decided to become a lawyer and what they like and don't like about it. Most lawyers would be more than happy to talk to you. As you listen to their stories, though, keep several things in mind.

Watch out for the generation gap. The longer one has been a lawyer, the more likely he or she will enjoy being a lawyer. Why do I say that? First, they have stuck it out when they could have switched careers long ago. This alone says something. Second, these lawyers are more likely to be at the top of their careers in terms of earnings, control of their professional lives, and power within their organizations. And third, the practice of law has gotten more intense, competitive, and businesslike since those lawyers rose through the ranks.

To get the most current information, after your discussion with a more experienced lawyer ask that lawyer to refer you to a newer lawyer. Someone they work with who's been out of law school five years or less. Then interview that lawyer too. The differences in perspective will tell you a lot about where law has been going.

Talk to as many newer lawyers as you can. The burdens and stress caused by changes in the legal profession are felt most strongly by newer lawyers. And newer lawyers are having the types of experiences that you are likely to have if you become a lawyer. Because their experiences and backgrounds are more likely to be similar to yours, their advice may be more helpful to you. As a general rule, it is a good idea to seek advice from those who are like you in background, goals, and work preferences. Their advice is most likely to focus on the issues that are important to you.

As you talk to lawyers about what they do, remember that there is a natural tendency to rationalize our own decisions. Including the decision to become a lawyer. Lawyers who are not especially happy with what they do may be reluctant to admit their mistakes. They may gloss over the negative aspects of their jobs. I have found that one way to get around rationalization of this sort is to ask the lawyers you speak with whether they want a close relative to follow them into the law. Someone who subconsciously dislikes what he or she is doing won't want someone he loves doing the same thing. So when someone says he wouldn't want a close relative to become a lawyer, find out why.

Finally, when talking to lawyers about what they do, get past the generalizations and into the details. How did this lawyer spend his or her day yesterday? Not how do they spend a "typical" day. What types of things are they working on right now? Not what do they "usually" do. Whom are they now working with, against, and for? Not whom do they "often" work with. It is harder to fudge or put a gloss on an answer if the question is specific.

Don't just run down a set checklist of questions. Listen carefully to the answers and ask probing follow-up questions.

Cross-examination

One of the cardinal rules of cross-examination is never ask a question if you don't already know the answer. During cross-examination at a trial, you're trying to control or undercut the testimony of a witness called by the other side by getting him or her to admit facts helpful to your side. That's not what you want to do in your informational interviews of lawyers. Instead, you're really conducting what lawyers call a discovery deposition. A series of questions intended to find out as much as possible about what a person knows about a given subject.

So follow the "rules" of a discovery deposition when conducting informational interviews of lawyers.

1. Do some investigation first. Look up the lawyer in *Martindale-Hubbell* to get a sense of his or her background. Ask him about his education and career. Seek out his career decision points and what factors influenced those decisions.
2. Engage the witness. Make the witness comfortable. Most people love to hear themselves talk, and love to talk about themselves. Especially to someone who shows a genuine interest in them.
3. Ask open-ended questions. Open-ended questions are designed to make your "witness" ramble on. Nod along with the answer to keep it going. A long, rambling answer will suggest further questions.
4. Ask pointed follow-up questions using parts of the lawyer's own

earlier answer. Probe. Make sure that you've gotten all the information the witness has on a given point before moving on. Watch
for clues in facial expressions, tone of voice, and body language for
answers that betray something unexpressed.

You want the lawyer you're interviewing to open up and confront
issues he or she may not have thought about before. Encourage this with
the kind of questions you ask. Here are some suggestions.

- If you could change three things about your job, what would they be
  and why?
- What was your most satisfying moment as a lawyer and how did that
  moment come about?
- What was your biggest disappointment as a lawyer and what did you
  learn from it?
- If you had your career to do over again, what would you do differently?
- And my favorite: Would you encourage a close relative or friend to
  become a lawyer? Why or why not?

You can come up with more questions like these on your own. Try to
get beyond mechanics and into issues of motivation, satisfaction, and
disappointment. Unless you're prepared with questions that get to these
deeper issues, you will get only superficial information.

Learning on the Job

Your interviews with lawyers will happen more spontaneously and more
frequently if you're working with lawyers. In addition, if you're actually
working with lawyers, you may be able to pick up information that no
lawyer would think to tell you. You'll see how a particular legal office
works and can use your own intuition to judge whether you'd enjoy
working in a place like that on a long-term basis.

Getting work in a law office before you go to law school isn't always
easy, but it can be done. The most accessible way is through a formal
intern or extern program run by your college. Some colleges have personnel who solicit alumni to take in a student over a midwinter or spring
break, or even over the summer. Thomas Pearce, preprofessional adviser
and assistant dean at the University of Virginia, describes how that
school's career planning and placement office helps undergraduates.
"We have an extern coordinator whose only job is to set up this kind of
thing. The coordinator makes calls off the alumni list or to other contacts
the office has. We'll even make cold calls to large law firms if a student

says that he or she wants to set something up in a particular part of the country at a particular time. Something usually works out. The students then spend a whole week from opening to closing in that law office, hopefully learning what lawyers do."

If your school doesn't have an extern program, or if you're not accepted into it, you'll have to find a job on your own. Ask friends, family, and any professors you know if they have any contacts at law firms or corporate law departments. Seek out students who worked with legal employers in the past. (Even if your school can't help you find a legal job, they may have a list of those who worked in legal jobs in the past.) The longer you're willing to work (most law firms don't hire nonlegal personnel for the summer) and the less pay you'll accept, the greater the likelihood you'll land something.

One great way to learn more about whether you'd like being a lawyer is to become a paralegal. I spent a little over a year as a paralegal after college and it was an enjoyable and enlightening experience. I worked long enough with one firm so that I got to know a handful of lawyers quite well. Not only did I see what their professional lives were like, I was in a position to ask questions about what they were doing and why. What their career paths had been like, and where they thought they were heading. And in some small ways, I was doing the same kind of work they were. So I could decide if I liked it or not.

If you can't land a paying job with a legal employer, think about volunteering at a law firm, corporation, government office, court, or bar association for a summer, or even for a month of the summer. The short-term financial sacrifice may be worth it in the long run. I had a college student help me out with a trial one summer. I got some free help on the case. He got to see what it was like to prepare and present a case at trial. His month of volunteer work was a good investment in his career planning.

Career Planning and Placement

I remember that when I was in college telling someone that you were going to the career planning and placement office was almost as bad as admitting you couldn't get a date for the big weekend. I guess it wasn't cool to suggest that you might need help figuring out what to do with the rest of your life. As a result, I didn't utilize a tremendous resource to the extent I should have.

The career planning office at your college offers you a variety of truly useful services. You may think that you've already narrowed your career choices down to law and something else. Why not find out what professional aptitude and skills assessment tests suggest you might like?

(There's a short description of one in Appendix C of this book, which should give you a feel for how they can help your career thinking.)

The career planning office can also help place you with a potential employer. That office probably coordinates any internship program run by your school, and collects information about various industries, professions, and companies. It's the place where employers will post information about job openings, leave sign-ups for job or informational interviews, and review résumés left on file by students. Take advantage of your career planning office. Get to know what types of information are available there. And get to know the folks who work there. They can tip you off to special opportunities open to only a few students.

Many colleges have specialized pre-law advisers. These counselors focus on helping you design an undergraduate course of study geared to preparing you for law, keeping current on the requirements for admission to law schools, and understanding the opportunities available in the legal job market. Track down your pre-law adviser early in your college years. You'll get helpful advice and will develop another potential source of contacts with practicing lawyers.

• II •

HOW TO BECOME
A LAWYER

· 7 ·

COURTING LEGAL SUCCESS

Okay. You've answered a bunch of questions about your interests and abilities. You've talked to all the lawyers and law students you know. You've gone to your career counseling office and have considered potential alternative careers. You took a career aptitude test. You've even read and thought about all the warnings in this book about folks who ended up unhappy practicing law—and you still want to go to law school.

Congratulations. You should now be more confident about your choice of a career in law. That confidence will help you over the bumps ahead. But, you ask, how do you go about distinguishing yourself from the other forty or forty-five thousand who will be starting law school the same year you do? What can you do now—what *must* you do now—to set yourself apart? How can you increase your chances of ending up with the position that makes you want to go to law school in the first place?

Merit Badges

While there are a sizable number of law school graduates who are struggling to find any job, another group has trouble choosing among all the choices open to them. Those in the latter group have collected a number of "merit badges," displayed on their résumés like the medals on a general's chest. These badges consist of degrees from prestigious universities, memberships in academic honor societies, seats on law review or moot court boards, positions of leadership in other student activities, and meaningful work experiences.

These merit badges don't mean that their owners will actually be better lawyers than anyone else. But the badges can get you in the door. Get you an interview. In the legal world, you will not get a job without an interview, so your first goal is to put together a résumé that will earn you a half hour with someone who hires.

Merit badges can do that. Think about it. The hiring committee of a large law firm may visit ten, twenty, even thirty law schools each year to interview students on campus. Usually the firm chooses which students it wants to talk with there. Countless other students who missed that cut or who go to schools not visited may send in their résumés. The firm will "call back" or "fly back" to their offices only a very small percentage of those applicants. Merit badges can cause that frazzled hiring committee member to read your résumé a second time, to decide to interview you.

How do the badges do that? They are screening mechanisms for busy lawyers. Law students have been repeatedly screened throughout their academic lives. They were screened by university admissions committees before they were accepted into college. They were screened during college by academic honor societies. Those who attained leadership positions in student activities presumably competed for them against other students, and were thereby screened again. The law school they attended screened them before admitting them. They were screened before becoming a member of the law review. Those who went on to clerk for judges were screened before being hired.

The busy hiring committee member doesn't have time to think too much about who you really are and what kind of contribution you would make if hired. And the hiring committee doesn't like to make "mistakes." So it's conservative. It looks for merit badges that say quality as surely as the USDA Choice label on the hamburger you buy. Merit badges such as Ivy League, Phi Beta Kappa, top-ten law school (don't worry, there are at least twenty or twenty-five "top-ten" law schools), law review, law clerk to the Honorable Judge So-and-So are the labels that busy lawyers use to find their new hires. If a new recruit doesn't work out, the committee won't be criticized. "Hey, don't blame me. The guy was Amherst undergrad, Stanford Law School, and clerked on the Seventh Circuit. How was I supposed to know?"

But what if you don't have as many merit badges as you might wish? Don't despair. Figure out which merit badges you can still earn, and go get them. The most important merit badges are the academic institutions where you received your undergraduate and law school degrees. Get into the best schools you can. Think about transferring into a better school after a superb year or two elsewhere. (Remember the advice I got from the Dean of Admissions at Yale. It wasn't bad advice. Virtually everyone coming out of Yale Law School gets a good job, even if they started law school elsewhere. In general, the "better" the law school you graduate from, the better your chances of landing a good job.)

Wherever you're at in school, look for badges to collect. Your grades may have suffered terribly that semester you broke up with your girl-friend or boyfriend. So Phi Beta Kappa is out of the question. But winning the history department's prize for best research paper or getting your short story published may be possible. In law school, if you don't make law review on the basis of grades, try "writing on." Most law reviews hold a writing competition to fill a few spots every year. If that doesn't work, join another journal that has open admissions. You may gain more experience in an area of interest to you—environmental law, international law, commercial law—and can collect a merit badge at the same time. If you can't get a job with a law firm for the summer after your first year in law school, don't go back to your old lifeguarding job. Seek a nonpaying internship with a judge or a prosecutor's office, or become a research assistant for a law professor.

Think creatively about how you can collect merit badges. And also about how to shape what you've already done into a merit badge. How to describe your experiences in a way that shows you have the skills a legal employer wants.

I met recently over breakfast with a first-year law student who wanted me to look over a draft of his résumé before he began looking for a summer job. He had put it together with the help of a software package, and it met all the "rules" he had been given about résumés: don't exceed one page, briefly describe significant extracurricular activities, list education, employment, and honors. This student had spent several years before law school working in a hospital, and about half the page described the things he had done there. Things he was justifiably proud of, like working in the emergency room. The problem I had as a lawyer reading his résumé was that it didn't tell me what this guy could do for me. When I mentioned this, his face lit up. "Pressure. I need to tell them how I handled pressure. A lawyer wouldn't care about the ER, but would care about how I reacted to the type of stressful work there—the same kind of stressful work I might face at a firm." Exactly. Take whatever you've done and translate it into skills that you will need in the *future*, not just skills that were important in your past.

The badges you most want to display are those that show you can use your mind, you've worked in a professional office before, you write well, and you can analyze complex problems or organize volumes of material. Those badges will help get you the interviews you want.

Beauty Contest

You collected your merit badges and lined up some interviews. Now what? How do you sell yourself to a legal employer? The obvious answer is by convincing those you meet that you'll make an excellent lawyer. While every employer has a specific ideal candidate in mind for each specific position, there are some general statements I can make about what makes a good lawyer. Here goes.

One of the most important things a lawyer or prospective lawyer must project is confidence. "We used to visualize how an applicant would look in front of a client or a judge," said a member of the hiring committee at one western firm. "Could this candidate persuade a person in a position of authority to change his or her mind?" To convince a legal employer that you would make a good lawyer, you must show confidence in yourself, and must demonstrate qualities that will instill confidence in others. Clients will be coming to you for advice. Unless the client has confidence in that advice, your effectiveness as a lawyer will suffer.

The qualities and abilities that combine to instill confidence in others are themselves things that prospective employers want to see in you. Intelligence. Clients don't often present you with easy problems. They can solve the easy problems themselves. They come to you with the hard ones. You have to be smart enough to solve them, or they'll take those problems to someone else. On another level, the employer thinking about hiring you wants to feel comfortable that you're smart enough to learn the ropes without constant supervision.

Judgment. Your value to a client—and thus to a legal employer—depends directly on how much they trust your judgment. Judgment is not easy to judge, or to develop. Judgment requires intelligence, common sense, experience, and a practical understanding of how things work. When I interview law students or lawyers who want to work at my firm, I often ask them to describe a failure or disappointment in their lives—and what they learned from it or what they would do differently if they had it to do over again. There are no right or wrong answers to these questions, but I believe I learn a lot about someone's judgment by how they answer them. A person who has learned from past mistakes really stands out as someone who's developed or could develop good judgment. On the contrary, a person who can't think of any mistakes or who wouldn't do anything differently doesn't impress me.

Your judgment will be evaluated on the basis of whatever clues you make available in your interview. How you respond to tough questions. How you describe your past experiences. The way you talk about your goals, and the way in which your résumé and transcript suggest you've attempted to meet those goals. In short, demonstrating maturity in the way you handle the interview is the best way to project that you have good judgment.

Show good judgment in every contact you have with that employer. Don't blow a good impression over lunch or dinner. Often your office interviews will be followed by what appears to be an informal social event. A chance for you to meet some lawyers in a more relaxed setting.

However casual it may seem, you are still being evaluated. "There was one guy who came through the office with high marks. We would surely have offered him a job," I was told by one big-firm lawyer, "except that at dinner he showed he really couldn't hold his liquor. He became loud and obnoxious. Frankly, we were embarrassed to be with him. After a show like that, why should we hire him? There are too many good people out there to take the chance."

Diligence. Sometimes it is not enough for a lawyer simply to be smart and have good judgment. Winning the trial, evaluating the potential contract, satisfying the regulatory authorities may all depend in the end on sheer hard work. Being prepared for any eventuality. Your clients want to know that you are willing to put in whatever time it takes to handle their problem effectively. Your potential employer wants to see evidence that you've put in the hard work necessary to overcome problems in the past. You can show this in many ways: you worked to put yourself through college or law school, you excelled in sports requiring hours of training, you wrote a lengthy and detailed research paper. Find evidence of your diligence and highlight it on your résumé.

Communications ability. Some people are simply more articulate than others. You may think that you can't do much to improve your communications ability. Not so. A big part of speaking well is knowing what you want to say. You can prepare for an interview, just as you prepare for a test. Some law schools put their students through practice interviews. If yours doesn't, have someone else interview you. Practice answering open-ended questions ("What type of law do you want to practice?" "What is your greatest strength?") as well as specific questions about your résumé.

Communication is a two-way street. Take some control of the interview. Don't sit back passively and wait for the next question. As a former hiring committee chairman at one of the country's largest firms told me, "A successful applicant shows some initiative in the interview by carrying his or her half of the conversation. It helps if he or she's done some research on the firm and can take a leadership role in the interview." You should practice techniques to get your interviewer talking about what he or she does. Lawyers generally love to talk—especially about themselves. There is no more articulate candidate than the one who listens intently to a lawyer rambling on about himself.

Be Prepared

When you've put something on your résumé, you must be ready to talk about it in detail. Your interviewer knows little else about you besides what appears on that piece of paper. If you can't talk in depth about the things that you've chosen to list there, the assumption will be that you can't talk—or think—in depth about much of anything. So prepare for the obvious questions. Think through in advance what it is you'd like to say about each item on your résumé. If you mention your college thesis on the sonnets of Shakespeare, reread it so that you can talk intelligently if your interviewer is a Shakespeare fan. Be ready to discuss how working for the poverty-law journal will be relevant to your corporate law practice. Have an explanation for the C you got in contracts.

Be prepared too for the obvious questions about what's *not* on your résumé. What did you do during the one-year gap in your work experience? Why did you decide to go to law school after working as an accountant for four years? Why are you interviewing with this company? Why are you interested in working in this part of the country? (This will probably come up if your résumé seems tied to another part of the country.) What type of law do you think you want to practice?

Written communication is also very important in most legal jobs. Have a good writing sample ready. Offer to provide it. Show that you are confident about your writing ability. Be prepared not just to regurgitate what's in your written work but also to react if you are asked to assume a different fact or to take a different point of view from what's in your writing sample. Legal employers want to know that you understand what you've written, not just that you can write well.

Personalize your communications to a prospective employer. A phone call to the firm or company will usually identify the person responsible for hiring. Send your letter directly to that person. Avoid "To Whom It May Concern." And don't forget to proofread the cover letter that you send along with your résumé. Lawyers are professional nitpickers. If your letter contains typos or, heaven forbid, you misspell the name of the lawyer you're writing to, it will reflect poorly on you.

Hiring the Veteran

Experience certainly helps. You can stand out if you've had a real job in the past. You've worked in an office. You know something about an industry. You've gained at least some perspective to bring to your position as a lawyer.

The way that most law students gain job experience is to work during the summers they are in law school. It's tough to get a job the summer after your first year, but try. If you can't get the job you'd really like, take one that gives you experiences you can use to promote yourself next year. Before putting it on your résumé, translate whatever job you get into a valuable experience in which you developed important skills.

If you can't get a paying job, take an internship with a governmental agency, work for a potential client, do anything that requires you to think and to interact with others in the workplace. You may have to do some digging to land an internship, but it's worth the effort. One prosecutor told me, "For our last three openings, we've either hired from within or hired lawyers who had interned with our office. No one wants to take a risk on hiring an unknown quantity with so many qualified people looking for jobs with us."

Internships (sometimes called externships when organized by law schools) are most useful when they are planned in a way that enables you to work toward a goal or to develop a skill. Cindy Slane, director of field placement programs at Quinnipiac College School of Law in Hamden, Connecticut, works hard to make the externships she supervises meaningful for her students. "A lot of legal employers think taking on an extern would be a great way to clean up their filing backlog and other 'grunt' work that isn't getting done. The structure and rigor in our program results in the supervising lawyers taking their mentoring roles more seriously." Cindy sends each potential externship supervisor a copy of the goals and objectives, as well as the course requirements, of the law school's extern program. "Each student must complete a detailed assessment of his or her legal skills and a learning plan for the externship semester. Students must identify what they hope to get out of their externships by choosing focus areas, such as management of legal work or improving legal research, and target skills they want to develop. Then they and their supervising attorneys must identify means by which the externship will develop their skills."

Not all internships are filled through law schools' externship offices. The federal government offers a variety of internships. Legal internships are available, for example, with the CIA, the FBI, the Supreme Court, and the White House. Contact your congressman or senator for help finding an internship. Most members of Congress hire interns in their own offices, and they may be able to help you locate an internship in an executive department. Your state government probably has internships available. Contact your state legislators to help with your search. Judges are also a fertile source of internships, especially state court trial judges, who often don't have enough research assistance.

Internships in the corporate world are described in Carol Carter's *Majoring in the Rest of Your Life* (The Noonday Press, 1995) and in *The Princeton Review Student Access Guide to America's Top 100 Internships*, by Mark Oldman and Samer Hamadeh (Random House, 1995). Or, as I've said before, seek out internships with law firms through your career planning office or using the old college connections with lawyers in your area.

The first hands-on legal work that many lawyers do comes during their involvement in a law school clinical program. Clinicals are law school courses that focus on a particular type of law for people who can't afford private lawyers—prisoners, the poor, those with mental disorders. Students learn the substantive law in the classroom, then apply it with real clients in the real world. Often in real courtrooms.

The full-time job experiences you gain before going to law school are just as important as your summer or internship experiences. Maybe more so. If you've been out working, even in another industry, capitalize on it. You have gained experiences that will give you perspective many other candidates will lack.

There is a tremendous rush by most law students to get into law school and to get on with their careers. Slow down. Law school will still be there in a year. Take a year "off." Defer your admission to law school or apply to law school while you are working as a paralegal or a bank trainee or a Peace Corps volunteer. It will make you a more interesting person, it will make you appreciate law school all the more, it will probably improve your law school grades, and it will make you more attractive to legal employers. If you jump from high school to college to law school, you may have proven that you are an excellent student, but most employers want someone who can approach problems in a practical, not just academic, way.

Real-world experience makes you much more attractive to real-world employers. One big-firm partner told me that future law students should take as much time off as possible. "Get experience in the real world. One qualification for being a lawyer is maturity and real-world experience, especially for those who go into business advisory positions. Some maturing experience in between college and law school is important to develop a work ethic and to learn how to relate to people in a work setting. When I interview candidates who went straight through from college to law school, I automatically mark them down twenty percent."

Taking time off gives you a break from academics and often a chance to have fun with other recent college grads. More important in the long run, it should provide perspective on life and work that will help you in law school and after. Glenn Fine, an academic All-American basketball player from Harvard, worked in Texas as a union organizer for the AFL-CIO before going to law school. "I wasn't the most beloved person in town. Driving around in a Chevette with Pennsylvania plates, I really stuck out like a sore thumb. But trying to organize steelworkers was a great experience."

Glenn later became a labor lawyer, representing unions, so his time off proved especially valuable. "As a labor lawyer, it was a real bonus that I had experiences with labor people and knew labor people. Someone once said to me that it will be helpful to know that you can stand up in front of a union meeting and address them not just as a lawyer but as a labor person." Glenn often recommends time off to others think-ing about law school. "Don't rush into law school. Take time off and you'll learn that being a lawyer's not that bad a thing compared to some of your other options. You'll understand better how privileged lawyers are. There's no heavy lifting, which is a lot different than working in a steel mill in Pearland, Texas."

It doesn't matter what you do between college and law school, but working in some law-related position will have the added benefit of furthering your examination of law as a career. If you work in a law office you should pick up an insider's knowledge about what practicing law is all about. What working conditions are like. What different types of lawyers do on a day-to-day basis. What kind of lawyers you might want to work with—and not work with. Your time working will also give you good substantive experiences that you can talk about on your law school application and in job interviews.

I'm convinced that those who take a little time off before law school also do better once they enroll. And doing well in law school is critical to your future success. Your first-year grades will determine whether you make law review, what kind of job you get after your first (and possibly second) year, and even whether you land a clerkship with a judge after law school.

Extra Credit

Another way to set yourself apart is to participate in any activity that shows your ability to write, speak, think, or just work hard toward a goal. If you write book reviews for a local newspaper, speak to elemen-tary school students about the evils of drugs, or play championship bridge or chess, it will reflect well on you as an applicant for a legal job. I personally respect accomplished athletes. If someone is a successful ice skater, swimmer, or lacrosse player, they have dedicated countless hours to improving their abilities. I expect that they will bring to their job the same qualities of determination and hard work that made them success-ful in sports. In short, take whatever you have and showcase it.

Finally, let's not forget the importance of just being an interesting and engaging person. Ben Webster, a partner in a small office of a San Francisco-based firm, looks for more than good grades when hiring new lawyers. "I also look to see whether the candidate has interests other than law. If not, I consider that a red flag. Also, with an office the size of ours, we make every attempt to have the interviewee meet everyone in the office. If one of my colleagues feels that he or she can't get along with the recruit, we won't hire him. It's important that the person seeking a job demonstrate that he can get along with others, be a team player."

Everyone who's made it to the interview stage has something going for him or her. Certain minimum qualifications have been met or you wouldn't be interviewing. So wow them. Show your drive, your special spark. Ask intelligent questions about your prospective employer—questions that show your interest in that employer. Everyone wants to be wanted. If you can articulate persuasive reasons why you really want to work for the particular employer, it can make the difference in landing the job.

Russell Jones, a name partner at Molloy, Jones & Donohue in Tucson, Arizona, says that he looks for honesty, integrity, and factors that indicate whether the person will stay with the firm if hired. "It's hard to predict loyalty, but indicators such as whether a candidate has held one job for several years are considered, as is his or her reason for becoming a lawyer. If her primary reason is to make money, then she probably won't stay with our firm forever because other, bigger firms can pay lawyers more than we can." In addition, he looks to hire lawyers "who will put their clients' needs before their own."

One way to figure out in advance how you stack up is to prepare your résumé now. Pretend that you're about to interview for your first legal job. How would you sell yourself? What would you emphasize? Where are the holes in your résumé? Think now about how to fill those holes so that you'll have an even stronger résumé before you really need to use it. As a means of setting goals, sit down now and write the résumé that you *want* to have when you're applying for real jobs down the line. Keep that ideal résumé in mind as you make decisions about how to spend your time, which activities to become involved in, where to seek employment, and what activities to pursue while employed.

For example, many states have law student intern rules that allow law students to present certain arguments in court. Research those rules and press your summer employer to let you give a real argument to a judge. Quite a nice merit badge for the résumé. Advance planning and follow-through like that will give you the focus you need to prepare for the job market of the future.

·8·

APPLYING YOURSELF

This chapter will take a look at the law school admissions process. That process begins long before you start writing "personal statements" and asking for letters of recommendation. Once again, it starts with you and what you want.

There are some obvious things you have to do to get into law school. You have to take another standardized test, the Law School Admission Test (LSAT). You have to subscribe to the Law School Data Assembly Service (LSDAS), the organization that forwards your transcript and LSAT scores on to law school admissions offices. You must experience the joy of completing law school applications: getting the application form in the typewriter so that it's not crooked, trying somehow to make the x key line up with those little boxes, and looking for gray "white-out" to fix the typos you make. Trying to come up with something, anything to say in those dreaded personal statements that will make you stand out without being too cute, too apologetic, too self-centered.

Before you do any of these things, you have to do some thinking about where you should go to law school and how to improve your chances of being accepted there.

The School for You

There are 176 law schools approved by the American Bar Association and still others that are not "accredited." (Stick with the 176.) How should you go about deciding which would be right for you?

Start by thinking about where you want to be when you graduate. If you want to work in a particular region of the country, focus your thinking about law schools on schools in that region. Some people will tell you that if you go to a "national" law school you can get a job anywhere. There's a lot of truth in that view. But if you know you want to work in one region of the country and you go to a national law school in another, you simply won't see as many of the potential employers that you want to talk to as you will if you go to a national or regional school closer to where you want to end up. If you're sure where you want to practice, you might even be better off going to a less prestigious school in that area.

The best place for you to practice will depend very much on who you are and what you want to do. But for an interesting, if very subjective, view of some of the better cities around the country in which to practice law, see Lawrence Savell's article in the March 1992 issue of the *ABA Journal*, "Looking for a New Place to Practice?" The article considers factors such as business climate, cost of doing business (e.g., office rents), potential rewards of law practice, and—for all but the largest cities on his list—the level of collegiality among lawyers. Savell's choices for the ten best cities for lawyers were: Austin, Chicago, Detroit, Indianapolis, Kansas City, Las Vegas, Louisville, New York, San Francisco, and Seattle.

Next, consider whether there is a particular course of study that you want to pursue in law school. If your reason for going to law school is to become an environmental lawyer, or an intellectual property lawyer, or an international lawyer, you'll want to go to a law school that has the course offerings and the faculty to permit you to develop that interest. If you want to practice at one of the large, national law firms or if you want to teach law, you'll want to attend the very best law school you can get into, regardless of geographic location.

Just as you did when choosing an undergraduate school, you will have certain personal preferences when it comes to picking a law school. There are big law schools and small law schools, and bigger or smaller isn't necessarily better. Harvard Law School enrolled over 550 students in its first-year class in 1993, while Yale Law School enrolled about 180. There are urban schools, suburban schools, and rural schools. There are law schools near beaches and law schools near mountains. Some law schools have very large classes, especially for first-year required courses, while others emphasize small class sizes. Some law schools have a more diverse student body and faculty than others. Your personal preferences on these issues are important considerations.

I remember some of the factors that made me want to attend Yale Law School. There was its strong academic reputation. That was important to me, but didn't do much to limit my choices—there are a lot of good law schools out there. More important to my choice were geography, financial aid, and level of competitiveness of the students. My girlfriend of seven years or so (now my wife) was from the Northeast and worked in consumer goods marketing. She wanted to be near her family and near good job opportunities in her field (New York), so she lobbied hard for Yale. Yale also offered a better financial aid package than the other schools I was considering. (It still was nowhere as cheap as Virginia, where I could pay very reasonable in-state tuition. But how many consumer goods marketing firms are there in Charlottesville?) Finally, Yale had a deserved reputation for being a low-stress law school. It didn't have grades in the traditional sense, had no class rank, and the law journal had a much more open membership than those of many other law schools. In the end, it was a good fit.

One thing I didn't think to look into, but which you should investigate, is the clinical programs and extern opportunities offered by the law schools you are considering. These programs, when run well, offer many students practical experiences that not only make them better lawyers but also improve their chances of getting a good job following graduation. For similar reasons, you would do well to investigate what joint degree programs are offered at the universities you're considering. The JD–MBA programs are popular and offered at many schools. Other joint degree programs include law–forestry, law–public health, and law–economics. These programs can really set you apart from the crowd, but they usually involve additional years of schooling.

Learn as much as you can about the law schools you're considering. Send away for the applications, even before you're ready to apply. The applications to law schools will tell you a lot about how a particular law school sees itself. The application brochures are marketing pieces, but they often contain loads of information about courses and faculty.

Refer to *The Official Guide to U.S. Law Schools,* which is put out by Law Services, the people that bring you the LSAT. That book profiles each of the 176 accredited schools, giving you an overview of the size of the enrollment, faculty, library facilities, curriculum, student activities, and special programs. Law schools are grouped by region, which helps you compare the schools in the part of the country you're interested in. *The Official Guide* also gives you information about LSAT and grade point averages for the applicant pool at each of the law schools, so you can evaluate your odds of gaining admission. Finally, don't overlook *Inside the Law Schools: A Guide by Students for Students,* edited by Sally F. Goldfarb. This is a good source of unbiased information drawn from law students themselves that will help you choose between schools.

A recent survey of 18,000 law students conducted by *National Jurist* produced some interesting results. This poll was not intended to determine which were the "best" law schools. Instead, it was designed to rank law schools by the level of satisfaction among their students. The top ten schools in student satisfaction, according to the survey, were:

1. Washington and Lee University School of Law
2. Seton Hall University School of Law

3. Notre Dame Law School
4. University of Texas School of Law
5. Washburn University School of Law
6. University of Southern California Law Center
7. Southwestern University School of Law
8. University of Toledo College of Law
9. South Texas College of Law
10. University of Washington School of Law

Similarly, Ian Van Tuyl's book, *The Princeton Review Student Access Guide to the Best Law Schools* (Random House, 1994), includes survey results for the top ten (and often also the bottom ten) for such factors as quality of life, competitiveness, and minority representation. All other things equal, you may want to consider the results of surveys such as these when you think about your law school options, but remember: past performance is not a predictor of future success, and the results of these polls vary from year to year. Don't depend too heavily on poll results. If at all possible, visit the schools you're interested in and do your own "polling" by talking with students there.

Ultimately, your choice of law schools will, as a practical matter, be constrained by how well you do on the LSAT and by your undergraduate record. But even if your academic record is not especially strong, you'll have choices if you do your homework.

Stop—Put Down Your Pencils— Turn Over Your Test Booklets

First there were the PSATs. Then the SATs. You may have thrown in some GMATs or GREs for good measure. Now it's time for the LSAT. The last SAT.

Few things are absolutely required to get into law school. The LSAT is one of them. Every law school approved by the American Bar Association requires that you take the LSAT prior to admission. In 1994, one man made news by getting into Yale Law School without going to college. He didn't have to go to college, but he *did* have to take the LSATs. They're required.

The LSATs are like a grown-up version of the SAT. There are five sections of multiple-choice questions. Each section takes thirty-five minutes, during which you blacken lots of oval spaces and worry whether you should mark three C's in a row even if you think each is the right answer. ("There is no penalty for guessing.") The test sections evaluate your reading comprehension, analytical reasoning, and logical reasoning. There's a half-hour writing sample at the end of the test. (Anyone who can write coherently at the end of that test *deserves* to go to law school.)

The highest possible score on the LSAT is 180. That's your goal. Just for paying for the test, they give you 120 points. So all you have to do is earn another 60. Shouldn't be too hard, right? In order to improve your chances of earning those last 60 points, you can do a couple of things.

The folks at Law Services (the ones who write the LSAT) will sell you old LSAT tests as practice exams. Six dollars each—three for fourteen dollars—plus postage and handling. Pick up a few of these and you can pretend you're taking the test at home. Time yourself. See how you do. (The six bucks per test also provides the answers.) There are also sample tests sold in paperback book form at your local bookstore. Surely someone will soon come out with a CD-ROM version, if it's not out already. Or you can take an LSAT prep course offered by one of the commercial outfits. In any case, you should at least become familiar with the format and instructions of the test and get used to the idea of testing under a time limit. The last thing you want to do is try to figure out each test section's instructions during your precious thirty-five minutes per section.

Speed and confidence may be the best thing that the LSAT prep courses teach you. I spoke with a lawyer who taught the Kaplan course for six years before herself going on to law school. "When I took the LSAT, my husband was on a business trip and I had been up for two days and nights with a sick child. I was terribly exhausted. Even in that condition, the techniques from the course had me completing the test faster than when I had taken it back when I was in college." She concludes that the review course "only helps people who really work. It won't help by osmosis. I saw people improve their scores dramatically —but only if they worked."

Another thing that's absolutely required to get into law school is to sign up with the Law School Data Assembly Service (LSDAS). You can't just send your grades and LSAT scores to the law schools you apply to. LSDAS has to do it for you. You send them your college transcript and give them information about yourself when you sign up for the LSATs. When you apply to a law school, LSDAS sends them your LSAT scores and your transcript.

The LSATs are offered in February, June, October, and December each year. Toward the end of your junior year of college, you'll want to contact the LSAT/LSDAS folks and start thinking about when to take the test. Many students take the LSAT in June after their junior year or in October of their senior year, to allow time to get their scores back before applying to law schools. Waiting until December or February of your senior year to take the LSAT may force you to apply to law school before you know how well you did.

Please Type or Print Legibly

Law school applications don't differ very much. Most of them want the basics: name, address, educational background, LSDAS registration number, something about your work and extracurricular activities, and the names of the people writing letters of recommendation for you. Doesn't seem too difficult until you look at the "checklist for application" and start thinking about the required "personal statement."

Here's the checklist in the 1994–95 application to the School of Law at the University of North Carolina at Chapel Hill, which is fairly typical: The application must be accompanied by:

☐ Application fee, $55.00. (Checks should be made payable to UNC School of Law.)
☐ Card #1, addressed to yourself with postage affixed.
☐ Cards #2, #3, and #4 (optional), addressed to your recommenders with postage affixed.
☐ Card #5.
☐ Cards #6 and #7, addressed to yourself with postage affixed.
☐ Two letters of recommendation in sealed envelopes.
☐ 1994–95 LSAT/LSDAS Matching Form available in the LSAT Information Book supplied by Law Services.
☐ One-page form supporting claim to resident tuition, if applicable.

Take your time and fill everything out properly. I'm convinced that how well you handle the logistics of the application process is taken into consideration by the admissions committee.

The most time-consuming part of the application—especially once you've pulled together all your dates of attendance and dates of employment—is writing your personal statement. This may also be the most important part of the application. It's the last chance you have to improve your odds of getting into law school. After all, your grades are what they are and your LSAT score is what it is. You either got to know some faculty members well during college or you didn't, so your letters of recommendation are beyond help at this point. But you still have to write that personal statement.

Your personal statement is your opportunity to convince the law school admissions committee that they should want you as part of the incoming class. It demonstrates how well (or poorly) you write. In fact, it may be the only writing sample from you that the admissions committee reads. So it could be your last chance to make yourself stand out. You want to showcase yourself as a potential member of the class both by what you say and by how well you say it.

But just what are the law schools looking for here anyway? A pure writing sample? An essay about your greatness? A self-analysis about why you want to go to law school (save the world, etc.)? An explanation for the low grade you got in freshman chemistry class? The admissions applications vary in what they tell you. The University of Kansas application simply says at the top: "One letter of recommendation and a personal statement are required." The point there may simply be to see if you read the application carefully. Item 30 of the application for admission to the Notre Dame Law School states: "A personal statement is required. Please append to application." This follows twenty-nine other requests, such as "List scholastic, honorary, or professional societies of which you are or were a member," "Have you ever served in the armed forces of the United States?" and "Have you ever been convicted of a crime?"

In contrast, the Harvard Law School application provides something of an explanation for what it wants the personal statement to be:

> To provide a context for writing your statement, we offer the following observations. The personal statement can be an opportunity to illuminate your intellectual background and interests. You might do this by writing about a course, academic project, book, artistic or cultural experience that has been important to you. The personal statement can also be an opportunity to clarify or elaborate on other information that you have provided in the application and to provide information about yourself and your achievements that may not be evident to the readers of your application. Because people and their experiences are diverse, you are the best person to determine the content of your own statement. It is for you to decide what information you would like to convey and the best way for you to convey it. Whatever you write about, readers of your statement will be seeking to get a sense of you as a person and as a potential student and graduate of Harvard Law School.
>
> We understand that it can be difficult to discuss oneself on paper, but our experience is that written statements are valuable in the selection process. Candid, forthright and thoughtful statements are always the most helpful. . . .
>
> Limit your statement to two pages, typed and double-spaced.

Any questions?

I still had a few, so I called up some law school admissions people. One admissions officer told me, "They really *do* get read. So applicants should spend some time preparing them. And they're called a personal statement for a reason. Be personal. It's the one chance we have to hear your voice. We want more than why you want to go to law school. We want to know what makes you unique. Tell your story completely, but engage the reader. We each have thousands to look at."

Jerry Stokes, Senior Assistant Dean of Admissions and Financial Aid at the University of Virginia Law School, offered fairly consistent advice. "Personal statements are key. They can keep you out. It's not promising if a personal statement is inane. And don't talk about a 'hot button' issue such as abortion—you'll immediately alienate half of the admissions committee. We're really trying to find out something about the individual. The personal statement is the only time the applicant gets to talk about himself or herself. It should be written to give us an insight into you. We want to get some idea of the person."

Because of the number of applicants to a school like the University of Virginia, the personal statement is extremely important. "Our applicant pool is five thousand. Two thousand of those are numerically qualified, and one thousand are very well qualified," Dean Stokes explains. With numbers like those, "grammatical errors or spelling errors in a personal statement can be devastating. And poems! You don't expect to get poems about a belly button in a personal statement, but I've seen it!"

Writing a helpful personal statement will not be easy, so allow yourself some time to complete it. You should also run it by a few friendly readers for comment—maybe the folks who are doing your letters of recommendation. What impression do they get from your draft statement? Is the tone right? Can they suggest improvements? As with any piece of writing, it may sound great to you when you read it to yourself, but always get a second opinion. Be sure that your writing conveys the message and impression that you want it to convey.

Don't Call Us, We'll Call You

What happens to your application after you send it off to a law school? Procedures vary from school to school, but there are some fundamental similarities. Most law schools have a faculty admissions committee. "This is important," I was told by one Dean of Admissions, "because it shows the level of seriousness given to the admissions process. Applicants should prepare their applications with a faculty audience in mind."

The faculty committee at one top law school splits up the undergraduate schools its applicants come from so that each member can become an expert about certain schools. "Each of us tries to really get to know ten or twelve schools," says an admissions officer. "We focus on things like: Which are the tough departments? Who are the hard graders among the faculty? What are the 'gut' courses? Which student activities are meaningful and which are not? How bad is grade inflation there? That way, an admissions reader who is inclined to admit a candidate can send an application to the school 'expert' for a second opinion. That second reader may say, 'Oh, no, this student took too many courses with easy graders.' We want to know how well the applicant really performed in comparison with candidates from other schools. A 3.4 average at a tough school may be more attractive to us than a 3.8 at a school with raging grade inflation."

Most law schools do not interview applicants for admission, in contrast to many colleges, which require interviews. The law schools that do interview are usually trying to decide between candidates fighting for the last few spots in a class. Still, applicants are strongly encouraged by most schools to visit and to sit in on classes.

When evaluating your application, most law schools take your undergraduate grade point average and your LSAT score and come up with an index. The index is used primarily to sort applications into categories: those very likely to be admitted, those very likely to be rejected, and the "great middle." The law schools and LSDAS (the people who run the LSAT) often trade information that enables the law schools to determine which types of information about you best predict your first-year success at their particular school. This permits individual schools to adjust their index to reflect actual results at the school. (If you want to get a sense of how the index is computed, and what index scores will get you into different law schools, consult *The Princeton Review Student Access Guide to the Best Law Schools*, which has these and other admissions statistics about most of the accredited law schools.)

How should you communicate with the admissions office? Most law schools have a procedure set up to let you know where your application stands. If you fill out all those postcards they send you with your application, the information starts coming back. Your application has been received. Your letters of recommendation have been received. And so on. Should you call the school to inquire about your status? "We're overwhelmed this time of year, with thousands of applications, each with three letters of recommendation. A lot of questions can be answered if people would simply read the literature," said one Dean of Admissions. "Still, if you have questions or if something about the process doesn't seem right, applicants should feel free to call. The ones who are a pain in the neck are the ones who call every day."

If you've collected your "merit badges," taken a challenging course load and done well in college, prepared for and excelled at the LSAT, complied with the logistical challenges of the law school application, applied to schools where you have a legitimate shot at getting in (plus at least one "dream" school and one "safety"), and written a thoughtful personal statement, you'll probably get one of those fat envelopes in the mailbox come April or so.

But if you aren't admitted, you should find out why. I didn't learn much as a result of my letter to the Dean of Admissions after getting rejected by Yale the first time, but you can be more direct than I was. I met one applicant who refused to take no for an answer. When she got a rejection letter from a top school, she called up the admissions office to find out what had happened. It turned out that the admissions committee had misunderstood something in her application. "One of my letters of recommendation said that I had left my job—without explaining that I left to move East and get married. It must have sounded like I left under a cloud. Once I told them what had happened, they reversed themselves and let me in. If I had just assumed that my grades weren't good enough or something, I would never have been accepted." Don't expect that many rejections will turn into acceptances with just a phone call. But if you're committed to going to law school, finding out the weaknesses in your application can only improve your chances of getting a fat envelope next time.

· 9 ·

LAW REVIEW

I had a law school classmate who described the competition to do well in law school in order to get a top-flight legal job as "a pie-eating contest in which the prize is a pie." Work your butt off so that you can get a job in which you have to work your butt off. Sounds like fun, huh?

It can be fun, but it won't be if you're caught off balance not knowing what to expect. One successful lawyer I spoke with was almost caught off guard by law school: "In August 1974, the day after Nixon resigned, I was hitchhiking to see my girlfriend one last time before starting law school. I had a copy of *The New York Times* under my arm and a guy stopped and said he'd give me a ride, but only if I read him the paper while he drove. After I had read him *The New York Times* from front to back, we started talking. It turns out we were both about to start law school together and would be in the same section. So he asked me, 'Are you going to brief cases? What about doing course outlines?' I didn't know what he was talking about, and it hit me that I was starting law school in two weeks and I hadn't *thought* about it. I said to myself, 'Holy shit! I'm going to law school. People are going to rely on me for advice and I can ruin their lives if I'm not any good. This is about preparing myself for the people who will rely on me. It *matters*!' I just didn't get it before then."

The purpose of this chapter is to take a quick look at what awaits you in law school and immediately thereafter: the bar exam.

The Burden of Going Forward

"It's time to confront the fact that law school is not law," says Charles Whitebread, a law professor at the University of Southern California Law Center. "Somebody's got to tell the kids that law school is just school. It's a great way to finish off a four-year liberal arts education, but it's got nothing to do with what you'll do for a living once you're out."

Perhaps for that reason, many law students who love law school hate the practice of law, and many who hate law school love practice. As one lawyer put it: "Because you're not working for a real client, the abstract nature of law in law school can leave you cold. Thinking about civil procedure in law school seemed meaningless. But abstract problems become much more interesting when thinking them through with a goal to make them part of a client's strategy that you helped craft."

Law school is not like college. Everyone who gets into law school did well as an undergraduate, but not everyone does well in law school. That's because the teaching methods are different, the subject matter is different, even the language is different. And especially the exams are different. "There's not enough feedback in law school," says Elaine Johnston. "My grades bore no correlation to how well I thought I had done on the exams."

Early on in your first year, you'll figure out some of the differences between college and law school. The most obvious is that there is a lot more student participation in even the largest classes in law school than is typical at most undergraduate schools. You will be called on. Not just if you raise your hand to interrupt the lecture. You will be called on by name, at random. (If you have an easy-to-pronounce name early in the alphabet, be ready on the first day of class.) When you're called upon, you will be expected to perform. State the facts of the case you read last night. What was the holding? (What's a holding? you're thinking to yourself if you're lucky enough not to be the one everyone's staring at.) How do you distinguish that case from the other one you read last night? Did both courts reach the right result? Why?

This ritual will be replayed every day of law school in almost every one of your classes. The process of live sacrifices of students by the professor in front of the class is called the "Socratic method." The approach of learning law indirectly by reading case after case and attempting to distinguish one from another (rather than reading sets of rules or "black-letter law") is called the "case method." The combination of the Socratic method and the case method can be a little daunting at first. You'll go home at night, read a bunch of cases for each of your classes, and often wonder what it is you are supposed to be learning. Some professors will pull it together for you eventually. Others won't. (That's why your law school bookstore sells commercial outlines of what you were supposed to be picking up from reading all those cases all year long. The outlines give you the black-letter law that may have slipped through the cracks as you looked for distinctions between decisions.)

This Is Only a Test

The uncertainty you may feel as a first-year law student will be magnified by the fact that you will probably get no feedback during the semester. At many law schools, in most classes there are no quizzes, no tests, no midterms—only final exams. You will work your tail off all semester reading cases and trying to pick up whatever it is you're supposed to be learning in a class and have absolutely no idea whether you get it or not. Did you ever think that you'd crave a pop quiz? Want another test? You probably will before your first semester of law school is over. Something, anything to let you know if you understand what's going on in class. Instead, you'll walk into your final exam and have three hours or so to write something in a test booklet that will convince the professor that you understood everything perfectly.

There is an art to taking law school exams. It takes some people, some very bright people, longer than others to figure it out. One lawyer put it this way: "Washington and Lee was a wonderful place to go to law school. But if I were starting over, I wish I had figured out that the name of the game was studying for exams. I naively thought it would be like college. The professor would tell you what you needed to know for exams. Not so. The faster you figure that out, the better you do in law school. What you need to know for the exam varies by course. In some, the class notes are critical. In others, it's more of a theoretical inquiry session. You should get a good book on that legal subject, usually one that's not listed on the course materials, and learn it cold. The clever people figured that out on day one. The people who just sat there and listened in class didn't have a clue how to do a super job on their exams. Law school is not like college at all in that regard."

One of the keys to taking law school exams, which often ask you to analyze legal issues buried in a lengthy and complex hypothetical fact statement, is "issue spotting." You'll get a certain amount of credit if you can identify what's important to resolving the legal problem presented to you. One lawyer I talked to recalls, "One of my professors told me that a law school exam is like 'turning over a rock, finding lots of bugs underneath, immediately spotting the biggest bugs of all, and nailing them as fast as you can. Every law school exam will have lots of issues. The key to success is spotting the biggest ones and writing about them in an organized, cogent manner in record-breaking time.'" The topics of issue spotting, time allocation, organizing an answer, writing an answer, and studying for law school exams are all discussed helpfully in *Success in Law School: Exam Taking Techniques,* by Charles H. Whitebread. Save yourself some agony your first year of law school by reading it early in your first semester.

My only additional advice on law school exams is to prepare yourself for what each of your professors is likely to throw at you. Ask students who took the course in past years what the final was like. See if they still have a copy. Or find out if that professor keeps a copy of past exams on file at the law school library, as is the practice at some law schools. Once you find out the type of test you're likely to get, and what types of information you have to be prepared to set forth on the exam, think about how you would attack it. If you have old exams, do a practice run. Be prepared and at least you won't be psyched out. Give the professor what the professor wants, and you'll get a better grade.

Survival Tactics

The first year of law school, especially the first semester, is the worst. The subject matter is new. The teaching method is new. The format of the exams is new. And you're taking courses that you did not choose to take. (Just about every law school has the same first semester: constitutional law, torts, contracts, civil procedure, and legal writing. Often criminal law and property law are required in the second semester.) Don't get discouraged. Every lawyer in America struggled to survive that same first semester. Just get through it. Band together with others into a study group, if that helps. By the time the second semester rolls around, you'll be more comfortable with the process. After a summer working, you'll realize that you *can* do real legal work. By the third year, you'll be bored with it all and eager to get out into the working world.

What you must do to survive is keep up with your reading, especially that first year. If you drop behind, you will get nothing out of class discussions and will go into preparation for finals searching for even the most basic concepts of the course. If you are keeping up but still feel lost, there may be a teaching assistant in the class who can offer some helpful advice or explain what was going on in a case you read. Teaching assistants are usually students who did well in the class the year before and who help the professor prepare for class and grade exams. The TA can be your friend. Don't be shy about asking a TA for help before you become hopelessly lost.

If there's no TA, ask the professor for help. They won't hold it against you. And it sure beats floating through the semester without a clue. The professor may seem mean because he or she is tying your classmates up in verbal knots during class, but they really are there to teach you and most do want you to understand what's going on.

Finally, don't shrink from class participation. Speak up. Take a position. Yes, it will be shot down or you will be asked a question that seems impossible to answer and makes you feel foolish in front of everyone.

But that's part of the process. You will emerge as a stronger student and more prepared both for the exam and for life after law school if you join the fray. Learn to think on your feet, to defend a position against critical questioning. After all, it's not unlike what you'll get from a judge or an opposing counsel out in the real world. There *is* a method to the madness of law school.

Just don't speak up in class *too* often. One Harvard Law grad described how some students in the larger classes played a game called "turkey bingo." "At the start of every class, we'd fill out our bingo cards with the names of the turkeys who spoke up in class every day. The idea was, when one of your turkeys spoke that day, you'd fill in that space. There was one guy who was known behind his back as 'free space,' because he talked so much that everybody put him in the middle. If you got five in a row in any one day, you got bingo and, to win, you had to say the word 'bingo' out loud. I remember one day a guy who sat in the back and never spoke up raised his hand. No one could figure out what was going on. We were discussing federal jurisdiction, and he said, 'If you had A and if you had B, then, bingo, you had federal jurisdiction.' The class fell apart."

If you can just make it through that first year, you're on your way. The second year allows you to start taking some elective courses, focusing on the substantive areas in which you may want to practice. But unless you're sure what you want to do on the outside, don't become too specialized. It's important to understand different areas of the law so that you can make connections and know when your future clients have problems that they don't recognize. To a large extent, you may want to pick courses by professor rather than by subject matter. If you find a professor whom you relate to and understand, take another course from that professor. So much of what you're learning is how to think like a lawyer. Don't punish yourself by taking a course from a professor you find difficult just to gain exposure to a particular subject matter.

The Screening Continues

Once again, in law school, the goal is to distinguish yourself. Remember, three years later you hope to be employed somewhere.

The best ways to distinguish yourself in law school aren't too different from the ways you tried to distinguish yourself as an undergrad. For future lawyers, the best way is to write. Get on a journal of some sort. If not law review, then some other journal. The educational system is faulted at every level for failing to teach people to write. Law schools are no different. Legal employers complain that law school grads can't do much of anything. They can't even write. Working on a journal doesn't mean you *can* write. But people will assume that you can. And it probably increases the chances that you will learn how.

Another important way to distinguish yourself is to get good work experience. (If you can't get an outside job, try to work as a research assistant for a law professor who's writing in an area of interest to you.) You either have work experience or you don't when you start law school. But law school gives you at least two summers (three if you end up clerking for a judge) in which to add to that résumé. You should obtain the type of summer work experience that will appeal to the type of employer you eventually want to work for. If you want to work in a corporation, spend the summer working at one. If you want to become a prosecutor, try to intern with a district attorney's office.

Sheila Madden, a prosecutor in the Arizona Attorney General's office, interned during her last semester of law school. "I summer-clerked at a firm and decided not to pursue a job there after graduation. Instead, I was determined to work as a prosecutor. I knew I had to work hard to secure a job with the state Attorney General's office. After talking to several people, I realized that by doing an internship I'd have a much better chance to get a permanent job offer there.

"In the internship program, I was assigned to work with one attorney. I shadowed him, attending all his court appearances, assisting with motions, helping to draft AG opinions, responding to correspondence, and participating in witness interviews. As the semester progressed, I was given more and more responsibility. I worked diligently and tried to make myself as indispensable as possible.

"I got a permanent job offer by dogging my supervisor and by getting to know as many people as I could. I didn't hole myself up in my office. If someone wanted me to go to lunch, I went to lunch. I played on the softball team. I went out for coffee. The efforts I made to meet people worked. I had numerous people who could vouch for me if and when I applied for a permanent job. Also, when you work for 'free,' some people feel they owe you something. So, when I asked for help landing a job, people were happy to help."

Most of you will probably seek work as a summer associate with a private law firm. There are lots of these jobs for second-year law students, but few for first-years. Summer programs differ among firms, but not significantly. The major differences are whether you will work in more than one of the firm's departments (e.g., trial, corporate, real estate, tax)—either by formally "rotating" during the summer or through less formal means—and whether you'll be assigned to specific lawyers for the summer. The less sure you are about what you want to do with your law degree, the more you should opt for the exposure to a variety of departments.

There are two schools of thought about where you should go for the summer. Some say you should, if possible, identify the city and even the firm you want to end up with. Most firms hire their permanent associates primarily from their summer programs. Others say you should go with the largest, most prestigious firm who will hire you for the summer. This is the keep-your-options-open school. The rationale is that, if you go with a big firm for the summer, you can still get a government job, a teaching job, or an in-house counsel position after graduation. My advice is: If you're sure you know what you want, go there for the summer. Your chances of landing a permanent position will be greatly increased. If you're less sure, you may want to go to a safe, résumé-building summer job.

Wherever you end up for the summer, treat it as a serious position. You may be wined and dined by some firms, but they will offer you a permanent position only if you excel at the work they give you. You want that offer even if you decide you don't want to return to that firm. Explaining to every other potential employer why you didn't get an offer from the firm you worked for last summer is tricky.

The Bar and Beyond

"Law school teaches you to read cases, spot issues, and make reasonable arguments about those issues. You are supposed to learn a way of thinking," says Mike Morrissey, who has taken and passed the New York and Arizona bar exams. "The bar exam is just the opposite. You are being tested on what law you know. The other difference between law school and the bar exam is that in law school, grades matter. The bar exam is pass/fail. You can't learn everything, so don't waste your time. Just learn enough law so that you won't be a danger to the community."

About the time you graduate from law school you will face the stunning realization that, having spent tens of thousands of dollars on a legal education, you have to shell out a few hundred more for the bar review course because you didn't learn half of what you were supposed to in law school. The reason for this is that most states want you to know their "black-letter law"—the actual statutes and judicial decisions of that state—before they'll give you a license. Most law schools—especially the national and regional law schools—want you to learn how to think like a lawyer rather than to memorize legal rules. In fact, the more prestigious the law school you attend, the less real law you're likely to learn.

The bar exam has two and in some states three components to it, as well as a separate ethics test. The "multi-state" exam is a standardized test used by all states. More ovals to blacken. Each state has its own state-specific test that can be multiple choice, essays, or a combination.

California has a third day because its bar exam includes two half days of practical drafting on top of everything else. Unlike other standardized tests, the bar exam doesn't travel well. If you want to work in a particular state, you have to pass the bar exam for that state. If you later decide to move to another state, you'll have to take another bar exam. (Unless you've been practicing law long enough to "waive in" to the other state's bar—and some states won't let you waive in no matter how long you've practiced.) This is really no fun, so try to get it right the first time.

I suppose it's possible to pass the bar exam without taking a bar exam prep course, but I don't know anyone who's actually done it. As a result, bar exam preparation is big business. As a third-year law student, you will be inundated with advertising for various review courses, each claiming to be the best. You will hear from classmates who have signed up (for pay) to be the class representative for different courses. Another source of marketing information. You will also hear lots of unofficial information about pass rates and differences in teaching materials of the study courses available in your state.

I'm not sure it matters very much which course you pick. Most of the established courses seem to do a good job of preparing students for the bar exam. One thing you should do, however, is to sign up for a course with a friend or two. Attending the bar exam prep lectures and taking the practice exams can be pretty depressing. It helps a lot to have a small support group to get through it together.

And don't overdo it. One lawyer I know was angry that he had gotten one of the highest bar exam grades in his state. "I overprepared. Took it way too seriously." Another lawyer recalls this advice from a law professor: "Continue to lead normal lives while studying for the bar or you will burn yourselves out and not be able to perform on the exam. If you don't believe me, take a plant that is used to sunshine and water, put it in a closet for six weeks, and then take it out. That's what you'll be like during the exam if you aren't careful."

Too Late to Turn Back Now

Next there's the problem of getting a permanent job. For lots of you, this will be simple. You will do well at your summer position. They will like you. You will like them. They will be hiring that year. You will go back there. Happy ending—or at least happy beginning. For all too many law school grads, though, getting a job is a real struggle.

I don't envy third-year law students who haven't gotten a job offer. They must struggle through their last year of law school in intense competition for the few positions not filled by graduates of a firm's summer class. It almost becomes a vicious cycle. Employers may look askance at someone who hasn't gotten an offer at the end of a summer, even if the simple explanation is that the firm where he spent the summer is cutting back on its hiring. Is there something wrong with this guy? Why didn't he get an offer from that firm?

You can avoid this problem only with planning and luck. When you are considering where to spend the summer, look at the statistics for the number of offers made from the summer class in the past. (These are published by a group called NALP—the National Association for Law Placement—and will be available in your law school placement office.) When you interview, try to get a sense of the firm's future needs for associates. Go with a growing firm, not one that's cutting back. Listen to the grapevine. Talk to someone in the class ahead of you who worked at that firm the year before—your law school placement office probably keeps records. After all that, hope for the best.

Even excellent lawyers are sometimes just unlucky. When a firm falls on hard times, its lawyers pay the price. One partner at a litigation firm in New York recalls just such a spell of bad luck. A graduate of Dartmouth College and the Yale University Forestry and Law Schools, he went to work for a law firm in New York that simply folded. The market was flooded with lawyers at the time, which made finding another job difficult. "It was very upsetting and shocking when the firm collapsed. And it was a terrible time to be looking for work. When I didn't find a position with a firm right away, I signed on with a legal audit company. It seemed interesting and paid enough to keep the wolves away. Then I registered with Special Counsel, a temporary lawyer service. If a firm needs temporary help for a big project, they call the temporary agency, interview you, and hire you as a temporary attorney." Through Special Counsel, he got a temporary job at a leading New York firm. "I poured myself into it. They offered me a permanent position, and now I've made partner. In the end it worked out well, but it was a much more tortuous route than I expected. These days it's very hard for lawyers to get jobs."

You can help your chances of landing a permanent job by concentrating in areas of the law that are more likely to need lawyers in the future. These "hot" specialties, which vary by region, are charted by legal magazines and newspapers every year, because they are constantly changing. Over the past four or five years, for example, bankruptcy work has gone from boom to near bust. Corporate work seems to follow the business cycle. Litigation generally stays warm, if not hot, since people seem to sue each other in good times as well as bad.

If you use information about hot areas of practice in your job search, be careful how you present your interests to a prospective employer. You may find more job offerings in the hot areas, but you should be able to give a persuasive reason why you're interested in a particular area. If an employer gets the sense that you're interested in the hot areas because they're hot, you may look a little desperate.

In the end, perseverance pays off. Most law school grads get jobs within six months of graduation. But it's getting harder and harder. In 1990, 90 percent of those graduating from law school had found work within six months. That rate dropped to 85.9 percent in 1991, to 83.5 percent in 1992, and to 83.4 percent in 1993, according to surveys conducted by the National Association for Law Placement. What's worse, only a little more than 70 percent of 1993 graduates found full-time *legal* work within six months of finishing law school.

· 10 ·

LOOKING FOR LAW IN ALL THE WRONG PLACES

This book is intended to help you find happiness in a legal career. But simply figuring out what type of law you want to practice and how to do well in law school will not guarantee you happiness as a lawyer. Finding the right work environment—an organization with the right structure, size, and personality—may be much more important. Will you have a supportive boss or one who's abusive and who takes credit for your ideas? Will you have colleagues who view you as the competition or who work with you as part of a team? Do you thrive in the formality of a large organization or feel swamped by the sheer size?

Just how important is the right fit? Consider this: You will spend many more of the waking moments of your life with your co-workers than you will with family and friends. Sad but true. Most of your life will be spent with people whom you'll meet for a half-hour interview, if at all, before starting your job.

One of the smartest things I did when looking for my first job as a lawyer was to shop for personality. I had worked for law firms in New York and Boston during my summers as a law student, and I assumed I'd return to a firm in one of those cities. But while I was completing law school and my clerkship for a federal judge, my wife was building a career at a company in Connecticut. She wanted to stay there, so I agreed to look at Connecticut firms.

I had to start from scratch, knowing nothing about any law firm in the state. So I asked around, and came up with a list of five highly respected firms. Some big, some small. Some handling mostly defense work, others mostly plaintiffs' cases. I applied and was called back to interview.

That's when I really went to work. I assumed that each firm had "good" clients and did quality work. So when I interviewed with them, I concentrated less on what they did than on the people who did it and the setting in which they worked. Would I like working with this person?

How do the lawyers here treat each other—and, more revealingly, how do they treat the secretaries, messengers, and others who work for them?

I kept my eyes open as I walked down the halls, looking for clues about the atmosphere of the firms. Was the lobby full of antique chairs I was afraid to sit in? Did lawyers put on their jackets when they walked around or were they in shirtsleeves? Most important, how did the lawyers and staff interact? No matter how charming, brilliant, or interesting I found the lawyers who interviewed me, I realized that I would be treated much like the secretaries when I first started work. If the lawyers were loud and demanding with the staff, I figured they'd be loud and demanding with me.

Looking for clues such as these, I narrowed my search down to two firms. Then I asked each of them to let me come back for a second interview. I figured the more people I saw, the greater chance I'd have of judging the overall personality of the firm. And that's how I chose where to work. Not based on "prestige" or profitability or starting salary, but simply on where I thought I'd best fit in.

After ten years, I've never wanted to work at another firm. Maybe I would have been happy at any of the five, but I doubt it. I'm convinced that interviewing for personality helped me find the right match. It can help you too.

Matchmaker, Matchmaker

If you've decided you'll like being a lawyer, the perfect legal job for you is out there somewhere. You just have to find it. How? By focusing your search on the types of job settings that are most likely to be ones you'd enjoy. You find that focus through a process of elimination. Eliminate the clients that you'd prefer not to work for and you've taken a big step toward finding the lawyers that you'd like to work with.

People who choose an adviser choose someone like themselves, someone they're comfortable with. For that reason, lawyers resemble their clients. Aggressive clients hire aggressive lawyers, corporate clients hire corporate-style lawyers, workaholic clients hire workaholic lawyers, entrepreneurial clients hire entrepreneurial lawyers. Generalizations are risky, but I'm willing to make this one. Someone who needs legal services usually wants a professional with whom they feel comfortable, someone who resembles them.

You can use this generalization in your process of elimination. If you feel uncomfortable with large corporations, you will likely feel uncomfortable with the (usually large) law firms that service those corporations. Not only will you be asked to do work that you might feel uneasy about; you will be doing it with people who don't share your reservations, and will likely be working in a firm that shares the corporate culture and values of the corporations it represents.

Similarly, if you think personal injury plaintiffs are simply hoping to win the lottery by blaming someone else for their problems, you'll be unlikely to want to work with the lawyers who represent personal injury plaintiffs. On the other hand, if you think personal injury plaintiffs are only seeking just compensation for injuries that should have been avoided, you should consider working at a plaintiffs' personal injury firm. Either way, if you can't stand up in court and project your sincere belief in your client, you will be neither effective nor happy as a lawyer.

The basic idea here is to eliminate what you find uncomfortable. If you're a woman or a minority group member, maybe it's a firm or corporation with few mentors for you or which you feel has shown insensitivity in hiring. If you went to public schools, maybe it's employers dominated by those who prepped at private schools. If you grew up in another part of the country, maybe it's a firm that expects you to have business contacts in the area. If you're a private person, maybe it's a company where the whole gang hits the happy hour after work.

You won't find information about these topics in the corporation's annual report or the law firm's hiring brochure. You may not gain that type of information from others who have worked at a place before you. You'll have to ask perceptive questions and keep your eyes and ears open as you interview. To help you out, though, let's look at some of the different settings in which you might practice law. If you can eliminate whole categories of jobs, your task of focusing in on what you might really like will be a lot easier.

The Options You'll Keep Open

I can't possibly describe all the career options you'll keep open by going to law school. I won't even try. Instead, I'll try to offer some general descriptions of the major types of jobs you might find after law school. At least then you should be able to figure out the areas that interest you most.

Hopefully, you've already put together something of a list of interests by answering the questions posed in this book. Use that list now to focus on the jobs in which you're more likely to find the right fit for you.

Private Practice

Private practice lawyers are lawyers for hire. They represent clients but are not employees of their clients—they are self-employed or employed by law firms. Private practitioners are the lawyers you usually see on

TV and in the movies. This is probably the kind of lawyer you thought you wanted to be when you first thought you wanted to be a lawyer.

Lawyers in private practice handle every type of legal issue imaginable, from arbitration to zoning, from banking to trusts and estates work. Aside from the subject matter of their practice, the obvious distinctions among private practitioners include the number of other lawyers with whom they practice and the types of clients they represent.

Going It Alone

"Working in a small or solo practice requires the ability and financial resources to survive the tough times as well as the good times," according to North Carolina solo Dan Read. "At the end of every month, after all the bills have been paid and I pay myself, there's always just a little cash in the till and I'm starting over again. With the responsibilities of helping support a family, this creates a fair amount of mental and emotional strain.

"The nice part of solo practice is being your own boss. I can pick my own cases. I can set my own schedule. My office is a two-minute drive from the kids' school. I can go down there for lunch when I feel like it. Last year I made most of the field trips they went on. I am a part of their school life in a way few other fathers are. That feels really good and fulfilling."

Dan works by himself, but is not alone. Nearly 263,000 American lawyers—about 45 percent of all lawyers in private practice—are solo practitioners. Often known simply as solos, these lawyers may be specialists in a particular practice area—real estate, divorce, personal injury litigation—or may be general practitioners. General practice solos were once quite common in years past, and still are in many smaller communities. Solo general practitioners are fairly rare in larger cities today.

Solos have the freedom to practice as they wish. They are their own bosses within their offices, responsible to no one but their clients. That freedom can be liberating, but can also be stressful and lonely. Solos often have no one else to bounce ideas off of or to share problems with. Solos reap all of the profits from their practice, but must bring in business by themselves and must bear all of the costs of the practice. When they are busy, solos have no one to help them meet obligations to be in two courts or with two clients at the same time. Perhaps because of mistakes born of this time pressure, solos are far more likely to have malpractice claims made against them.

You shouldn't overlook solos as potential employers. Many solos or two- or three-lawyer firms would like to grow their offices into larger firms. That's something Peter Brown did quite successfully. "My friend

Richard Raysman had gone to MIT, and after college he worked for IBM in systems engineering while going to law school at night. After holding a corporate position, he opened a solo practice in Manhattan. It was crazy because he had no clients. He kept encouraging me to join him, but the time was never right." Peter, who had been working with a medium-sized firm, eventually agreed to sign on.

"We were subletting space from a four-lawyer firm. There was a partner's office and a secretarial station. Because Richard had the more established practice at the time, he got the partner's office and I got the secretarial station. But the deal was, if I was bringing a client to the office, in order to impress them, we'd switch and I'd use Richard's office that day." Brown and Raysman began building a practice in computer law, then an unestablished area of the law. They soon added another partner. "We told Julian Millstein: you can leave Hughes Hubbard, give up your partnership track, cut your income in half, and take a very modest share of any profits we make, but see your name on the door. He bought the deal, and I made sure that the brass plaque had his name on the door from day one."

The name on the door was Brown, Raysman & Millstein. In 1979 the firm had two lawyers. Today it has fifty-five lawyers working at offices in New York, Hartford, Newark, and Los Angeles. And Peter Brown no longer sits at a secretarial station.

As an associate to a solo or very small partnership, you'll be getting in on the ground floor. Over the immediate term, you could help relieve some of the time pressure an individual practitioner faces. You will not likely earn the salary you could with a large firm, but you will likely get more practical experience earlier and have a better chance of becoming a partner. Be careful, though. If you associate with a solo, you want to be sure that you've chosen a good mentor and entrepreneur. You want to find someone who can build a successful practice while teaching you well, rather than someone who will merely throw you in the middle of the lake to see if you can swim.

Of course, you could simply hang out a shingle and become a solo yourself. You'd then enjoy the benefits of your own practice. But becoming a solo is not a decision to be made lightly. Too often, it is made out of desperation because no other job is available. There are many books written about going out on your own. Read them before you do so. And consider the significant start-up costs, the difficulty in finding enough paying clients, and the problems of learning to practice law without a mentor.

"There are four phases to going out on your own," according to Douglas Gall. "Phase one, you spend a ton of money to get set up. Phase two, you have no paycheck and you're not making enough to pay your bills.

Phase three, you start getting work, but when it's plaintiffs' work you can't charge for it up front, so it takes a couple of years to get a decent cash flow. I've made it through the first three phases now and, hopefully, phase four is when you begin to make a decent living."

The Firm

"Let's face it, life in a law firm isn't always a picnic. But as long as I'm practicing law, that's where I want to do it," says Kent Sullivan, managing partner of Houston's McFall, Sherwood & Sheehy. "The hard part of firm practice these days is convincing the other owners of the firm— the partners—that they can't do it the way they've always done it. You've got to be proactive, not reactive. You've got to have a coordinated effort to identify and obtain business opportunities, and to marshal the resources so that you can adequately represent people. What you can't do anymore is function as a group of solo practitioners. Firm lawyers have got to be willing to cooperate with each other. The firm has to be a group of creative and interdependent lawyers."

All law firms are, in essence, collections of lawyers that work together in differing degrees of coordination to represent clients. Beyond that, it is difficult to generalize. Areas of practice, type of clients, form of firm governance, and nature of compensation systems all vary greatly across firms. And most of these characteristics are not apparent to the prospective employee of the firm. As private entities, little public information exists about law firms. There is no annual report you can read to learn more about a firm. You'll have to do your own investigating.

The most obvious way to distinguish among law firms is by their relative size in a particular locale. Generally, the larger a firm in any community, the more "prestige" there is in being associated with it. People in the community will have heard of the firm. The larger firms are likely candidates to handle the legal work for the larger corporations in the area. Larger firms generally charge more for their services (thereby pricing themselves out of certain types of lower-budget work). These firms generally pay their associates better. Often the larger firms earn the resentment of other lawyers in town. As is true with any type of organization, larger size leads to greater bureaucracy and makes it increasingly difficult for individuals to make a dramatic impact.

Smaller firms are usually more freewheeling. The rules are often less formal. The time it takes to become a partner, for example, is usually shorter, and promotion to partner may be decided on a case-by-case basis. Smaller firms are often more directed and entrepreneurial. They sometimes can react—and have to react—faster to changes in the marketplace than larger firms. Small firms generally have to rely on the personal contacts of their lawyers, rather than the firm's name, to bring in business.

Many large firms have smaller offices in cities around the country or the world. Your fit at a particular firm may depend on which office you work in. Would you rather work in the main office and be at the political center of a firm, or would you be happier at a smaller, perhaps less formal office? I work in a small office (about thirty-five lawyers) of a large firm (over two hundred lawyers) and I think that I've found the best of both worlds. I enjoy the reputation, resources, and client base of a large firm, but I work in an office that has the informality and collegiality of a small firm.

Style of firm governance is another aspect for you to consider in deciding whether a particular firm is right for you. Whatever size a firm may be, it can be run as an autocracy, an aristocracy, or a democracy. No lawyer is likely to describe his or her firm as anything other than democratic, so you'll have to look for subtle clues to figure out the real story. The general form of partner compensation will tell you a lot. If partners are compensated primarily on the basis of such factors as seniority with the firm, without significant distinctions among partners of the same relative experience, the firm is likely to be relatively democratic. If partners "eat what they kill"—that is, get paid based on the amount of legal business they bring into the firm—the rainmakers are likely to rule everyone else. (Be careful about raising these sensitive issues in an interview. Better to pick up this kind of information as a summer associate or from a former summer associate.)

Firms can specialize in certain types of law or can be general practice firms. Even firms that hold themselves out as general practice firms may practice predominantly in one or two fairly specialized areas. You should find this out, because it may affect your fit with that firm. If you end up in the predominant department, you will more likely become a specialist. If you end up in a smaller department, you will likely be more of a generalist.

One of the downsides of life in any private law firm is the risk that you and your time will be treated as simply a factor of production. As one big-firm lawyer put it, "I feel sometimes like my mind is for rent. Anybody can walk through that door and hire my mind for whatever *they* want to use it for. I don't have the freedom to do what I want with my brains." After all, a lawyer's advice, usually measured by the time it takes to provide it, is what the lawyer sells. The more time spent on client matters, the more money the firm will bill its clients. The system can lead to intense pressure to work—and bill—incredibly long hours, month after month.

Long hours are standard at most law firms—and represent a common source of complaint among law firm lawyers. "The large deals are out-rageous," says one lawyer who worked in the corporate department of an Arizona firm. "The assumption by everyone involved is that this is the most important thing in life, so the hours are unbelievable. In one deal I worked on, we had four days to close the transaction. I probably had twelve hours of sleep in four days. I would work until 3 or 4 a.m., make the half-hour drive home, and return by 7 a.m. On the third day, I didn't want to lose the hour of sleep I gave up by commuting home, so I decided to stay near the office, but I didn't have a change of clothes. I borrowed a dress from a co-worker and my secretary's belt and coat for work that final day of the deal."

Keeping track of your day by six- or ten-minute intervals is a pain. What's worse, though, is the effect the billable-hours system has on a lawyer's personal life. There will be direct and indirect pressures on you to work evenings. You may have to fight to keep weekends to yourself and your family—and doing so may affect your standing in the firm.

One former associate at a midsize New York firm planned a weekend rendezvous with his cross-country girlfriend. He cleared the trip with the firm and purchased nonrefundable tickets to leave New York at 4 p.m. Friday and return 9 a.m. Monday. As he was leaving to catch his flight on Friday, the chair of the litigation group asked for a memo by Monday morning. When the associate reminded the partner that he was flying out of town for the weekend, the partner suggested that he read the cases on the plane out and write the memo on the return flight. "I didn't even have time to collect the cases before I left for the visit, so I flew cross-country, and ended up spending eleven hours on Saturday in a law library with my girlfriend. The partner who assigned the memo didn't care how much of my personal time it took so long as the memo was on his desk Monday morning."

The pressure to work harder and bill more and more hours takes its toll on some lawyers. I spent a summer during law school working for a large New York law firm. I did fascinating work, met lots of interesting people, and was wined and dined by the firm's partners. It was heady stuff. I decided not to work at a large New York firm after graduation, however, in part because of a conversation I overheard that summer. My office mate was a fifth- or sixth-year associate. One day he commiserated to a friend that his four-year-old had asked his wife whether Daddy still lived with them. When his two-year-old wanted to play with Daddy, she'd open the shower curtain to look for him—because the only time she saw him was during his morning shower. That associate saw the light and moved to another firm, in a smaller city. I saw the light too.

At some firms, travel is a given. After graduating near the top of her class at New York University Law School, Kaare Phillips clerked for a federal judge. Then she joined a large, prestigious New York City law

firm. Her first assignment took her from New York to the West Coast—
for ten months. "I didn't consider it to be all that bad a thing," she
recalls. "That's just one of the things you sign on to when you join a big
firm. I actually think I got better exposure on that case than I would
have if I'd stayed in the office. And my husband jokes that it was the
best time in our marriage. He got all these weekend trips to California
where he'd drive around in my sports car with the radio blasting while
I worked."

As you think about where you'd like to end up, consider how joining
a particular firm will affect your career mobility. When you start with a
firm, you're on the "partnership track"—working to become a partner.
Most law firms hire more new lawyers each year than they can possibly
make partner when the time comes. (The time, by the way, varies significantly. Usually it's between five and ten years of practice. Don't forget
to ask.) Thus, many of a firm's associates will leave the firm someday.

You should find out where a firm's "alumni" go, either when they
decide to leave or when they don't "make partner." At most law firms,
the partnership track is an "up or out" system, as in receiving tenure as
a college or university faculty member. (The fights over who makes partner can be just as bitter as tenure battles.) The usual choices for those
who leave law firms are to join another (usually smaller) law firm or to
go "in-house" with a corporation. Some lawyers plan to spend only a
few years at the first firm they join. They join the largest, most prestigious big-city firm they can in order to "get experience" before returning
to their hometown. (This is just another form of keeping your options
open.) I question this approach. Your experiences at one firm or in one
location may not be readily transferable to another—and may not be
valued when you move. Thus, you may end up starting all over again
in a new place. If you know where you want to end up, go there.

If you leave one firm to go to another, you're an actual or potential
competitor. But if you go in-house, you're an actual or potential client.
The difference can have interesting consequences. When Bob Barber an-
nounced that he would leave a large D.C. firm to go in-house at AT&T,
"I had partners who'd never spoken to me before suddenly chasing me
down the halls to wish me good luck."

What keeps many associates working at a firm is the prospect of making partner. In addition to increasing your job security, making partner
usually increases your compensation. Instead of receiving a salary and/
or bonus, partners receive a "draw" or "share" of the firm's profits.
When a law firm does well economically, the firm's partners can do very
well indeed. With few exceptions, the best-paid lawyers are partners in
large law firms. A *National Law Journal* sampling of profits per partner
at a variety of large firms around the country shows most between
$200,000 and $400,000 in 1993.

In-House

"Although I have many deadlines, I have more control over the situation because I manage my time and can determine if the deadlines are real," says Karen Dickinson, an in-house lawyer with Honeywell. "Usually, the hours are more predictable than they are in private practice and I have more freedom to do whatever I want outside of work. When I was with a law firm, I was supposed to spend my 'free time' doing pro bono work, helping recruit new lawyers, and attending firm social functions. I have more decision-making authority than I did in private practice. Another subtle, but important, difference is that I associate with businesspeople on a daily basis and have in-depth knowledge about certain aspects of the business, so my work has a more practical focus to it than it did in private practice. But there are drawbacks to being in-house. The working facilities are not as good, the clerical support is limited, the money is not what it would be in private practice, and I am somewhat isolated from the legal community."

Despite the differences that Karen points to, practicing law in-house at a corporation is often a lot like private practice—without the time sheets. In-house lawyers do all the things that outside lawyers do—from drafting contracts to trying lawsuits—only they do it for a single client, their employer.

There is as much variety among corporate legal staffs as there is among private law firms. Some corporations have only one legal employee—the general counsel. Others have huge, far-flung departments. AT&T, IBM, and General Electric each employ about 370 lawyers in-house. At that size, those corporate law departments would rank among the forty largest law firms in the country.

Personalities among corporate legal staffs also vary. Some are intense. Others laid-back. Some are dominated by powerful individuals. Others operate on a team concept. Some keep most legal work for themselves. Others farm most of it out to private firms. Some hire only specialists, while others search for generalists.

Since each corporate legal department is part of a corporation, such departments tend to handle the type of legal problems shared by all corporations. Thus, most publicly owned corporations have in-house lawyers who specialize in securities law—compliance with the many laws regulating public disclosures that must be made about their operations. Most also have lawyers experienced in legal issues relating to finance—loan and credit agreements, stock offerings, and bond issuances.

Many corporations employ lawyers who advise them about the highly regulated areas of employment and pensions. Corporations, of course, are employers of large numbers of workers, and employees have many rights in today's workplace. Rights to be free of discrimination and sexual harassment, rights to unemployment and worker's compensation, and rights to retain their jobs if they are forced to be away from work because of pregnancy or certain medical conditions. It takes experienced and knowledgeable lawyers—often working with a human resources department—to stay on top of the rapidly changing employment laws.

Most corporations hire in-house lawyers either to manage or actually to litigate lawsuits. Disputes frequently arise between corporations. Contract issues, copyright or trademark infringement, and unfair competition are just a few of the myriad disputes between corporations. Corporations also engage in litigation with governmental entities: tax disputes, regulatory issues, and even criminal prosecutions are examples of litigation between government and corporations. Finally, corporations are frequently targets of lawsuits brought by individuals—product liability claims, environmental contamination problems, and simple slip-and-fall cases are among these. Pick up the newspaper and you're likely to see an example of this, such as the woman who successfully sued McDonald's after she spilled scalding coffee on herself.

When a corporation sues or is sued, it will usually have one of its lawyers either handle or supervise the litigation. In the former case, the in-house lawyer does exactly what a private practitioner would. In the latter case, the in-house lawyer works with a private lawyer to develop a litigation strategy for resolving the case as cheaply as possible for the corporation. The in-house lawyer reviews and approves actions taken by the private lawyer. Generally, the in-house lawyer is the client representative most closely involved with private counsel.

Finally, in-house lawyers deal extensively with the particular legal problems faced by the companies in their particular industry. A trucking company lawyer will need to know the state and federal regulations governing transportation. A cable company lawyer will keep abreast of statutes and regulations governing the cable industry, as well as court decisions dealing with free expression and libel. A lawyer for a company with significant foreign operations or trade may need to know the laws governing exports and imports, as well as the substantive laws of the foreign countries where it operates.

Obviously, in-house lawyers who deal with legal issues that are common to many corporations—employment, securities, litigation—will have greater career mobility across industries. Those who specialize in problems of a particular industry will have less mobility outside their own industry.

The benefits of in-house practice include competitive pay, excellent benefits (insurance, profit-sharing, vacation, and pension plans are usually superior to what you get at law firms), often less stressful work, no time sheets or billing targets, and the opportunity to make a transition into a business rather than a purely legal position. "I feel more part of a team, more like I'm helping create something here than I did at my firm," says one in-house lawyer. In addition, although there are pressures on an in-house lawyer to advance within the corporate structure, that pressure is usually less intense (and less closely tied to a set schedule) than the pressure to make partner at a law firm. "There's no up-or-out here. But you don't always know how you're doing. There's no sense of career progression. You can stay at the same basic level for a long time," according to one corporation lawyer.

Other downsides include: (1) potentially greater corporate politics (one lawyer told me about periodic "territoriality" meetings at which in-house lawyers jockeyed with lawyers from other departments for desirable responsibilities), (2) risk of downsizing or layoffs (the corporate legal department is usually an expense center, not a profit center—even if it saves the corporation money in the long run), (3) a difference in the types of legal issues in which you'll be able to be directly involved, (4) heavy travel schedule and risk of transfer to another geographic location (especially if you work for a large, far-flung corporation), and (5) difficult time constraints where business managers need advice "as soon as possible." One corporate lawyer described the feeling of giving advice on the run, shooting from the hip: "There's no time to do research and be sure you're right. So you give the advice you think is right, but you always have to qualify it—and hire outside counsel when you absolutely have to be right."

How can you get an in-house job? Some in-house positions are open to those right out of law school. Interviewers will come to your law school. Other times, corporations hire from the ranks of law firms, looking for individuals with specific types of expertise or experience. (Quite often, corporations hire lawyers from firms representing them, since they have had a chance to work with and get to know those lawyers.) You should investigate the potential for advancement at a particular corporation for lawyers with and without prior experience before signing on with a particular company.

Working for the Government

"The work here is more interesting than in private practice. A private dispute is certainly interesting to the clients involved, but here there's a broader purpose and a broader effect to whatever you do," one government lawyer told me. "One of the people I worked with on the campaign put it very well. He told me, 'You worked your ass off to get Bill Clinton elected, and now you want to make policy.' It's true. In my own way, I get to push things along and promote ideas I believe in. For twelve years we had a lot of lousy policies; now it's being corrected and I'm part of it. That's a feeling you don't get in a private law firm. It's heady stuff but you realize it's only for a short time."

Governments at every level—local, state, and federal—hire lots of lawyers. Some, like the person quoted above, are in policy-making positions. Many others function in more traditional lawyer roles. The most visible government lawyers are prosecutors and judges. But government lawyers practice all kinds of law and are found in many places besides the courtroom.

Prosecutors come in many stripes. If you fight a speeding ticket, your adversary will be a prosecutor. If you pollute a nearby river or fail to pay your taxes or hire an illegal alien, your adversary could very well be a prosecutor. In fact, if you fight the denial of social security benefits, a "prosecutor" from the U.S. Attorney's office will likely oppose your efforts. There's even a special corps of military prosecutors. Prosecutors are becoming involved in a broader and broader range of disputes because an increasing number of statutes carry criminal penalties—including criminal penalties against corporations.

Prosecutors try cases. If you want to gain trial experience, becoming a prosecutor is one of the best ways to do it. Because criminal defendants have a right to speedy trial, criminal trials often take precedence over civil trials. In fact, some lawyers are concerned that our federal courts are becoming the federal criminal courts because criminal cases are crowding out civil cases.

Because many lawyers want the trial experience that comes with being a prosecutor, the competition for prosecutorial job openings has increased dramatically. A federal prosecutor in one western state told me, "For two open positions in our office, we received 800 applications." The story is the same back East, where another federal prosecutor's office received 1,200 applications for six spots. Some prosecutors offices now require that you have legal experience before they hire you. So some prosecutors start out in private practice.

"I had to learn the difference between being a litigator and being a trial attorney," says Mike Morrissey, an Assistant U.S. Attorney. "A litigator may prepare cases for trial, but does not necessarily get to try cases. In fact, most litigators at private firms spend the majority of their time doing pretrial motions, discovery, and research. For example, as a litigator at a firm in New York City, I joined a big case that had been in progress for three years. In one year of working on the case, I took part of one deposition. Five years after I left the firm, the case went to trial —and everyone was surprised that it did. That's eight years to get to trial with six lawyers working the case on one side alone. As a prose-cutor, I did eight solo trials in two years—and knew people working in the area of violent crime who had many more trials in that time period."

But prosecutors are far from the only government trial lawyers, let alone the only government lawyers. The government also employs a cadre of public defenders. These lawyers are available to indigent crim-inal defendants at government expense. Part of the "Miranda warnings" that we hear repeated so often on cop shows on TV ("You have the right to remain silent . . .") is the offer to have the services of a lawyer pro-vided free if you cannot afford to hire one. Public defenders are the lawyers who provide that service. Like prosecutors, public defenders spend a great deal of time trying cases.

Government trial lawyers also defend the government against civil suits. Claims against the government raise issues of employment law, constitutional rights, prisoners' rights, zoning, tax, denial of govern-mental benefits, and simple negligence or personal injury cases.

Governments run the courts, and the courts employ many lawyers. Most obviously, the government employs judges. Getting "hired" as a judge is a little different from getting hired as almost any other kind of lawyer. It's been said that federal judges are lawyers who knew a sen-ator. Depending upon the state's laws, state and local judges are lawyers who either knew the right politician and were appointed to their posi-tions or were themselves successful politicians elected to judgeships.

Courts and judges employ lawyers as clerks. A judge's law clerks are usually top law school graduates who work with a judge for a year or two following graduation. Judicial clerks get a brief, but exciting, chance to participate in the judicial decision-making process. They help the judge research legal opinions, assist the judge with trials or appeals, and get to discuss the judge's thinking about pending cases in the privacy of the judge's chambers. Court clerks do any number of things, from re-searching motions and writing draft opinions to various administrative functions that keep the courts working.

In recent years, the courts have also employed various types of me-diators with increasing frequency. Christopher Goelz is a court mediator for the U.S. Court of Appeals for the Ninth Circuit (the far western part of the United States) in Seattle, Washington. That court employs five other court mediators, who work in San Francisco. Official mediators attempt to resolve cases without the need for further litigation or court proceedings. "In my view, I'm helping to streamline or eliminate un-necessary litigation. In some cases, I'm helping people settle the under-lying disputes that led them to court and providing an alternative way for people to have the court system respond to their dispute. Often the clients have lost control of their cases to their lawyers by the time a case is on appeal. After a trial, the client asks if they have anything to appeal and the lawyer says yes. The dispute then becomes very legalistic. I try to give the clients another 'day in court' and make sure that they come out of the process with a good feeling about the judicial system."

Chris started out in private practice, but prefers his position in government. "I have a lot of control over my workload and my day. It's easier to smooth out the peaks and valleys in my work than it was in private practice. I can plan vacations and my life in a reasonable way— a true luxury in the law biz. You can get a little bored with your cases in private practice because they drag on so long. Here, there's an incredible amount of turnover. I read the cases, hear the stories, and do what I can to resolve them. Things either work out or they don't, but I get to move on to the next case. The parties either settle or the case gets briefed and the judicial system does what it does. Litigation can move people further apart. It has its own emotional cost that is irreparable. But I try to bring a slight civilizing influence to it."

Government lawyers not only help interpret and enforce laws; they also help make them. Legislatures hire lawyers to advise legislative committees. These lawyers help draft the actual language of statutes—and provide important insights and analysis of the effect of draft legislation. "I've gotten more understanding about why the law is sometimes drafted as badly as it is," says Richard Orr, who left a partnership at a respected firm to become counsel to the Speaker of the Connecticut House of Representatives. "A statute may not be clear, but if people understood what it says, you'd never get seventy-six votes for it."

Richard has a varied background in the law. He was on law review at NYU Law School, clerked for a federal judge, and spent three years at Arnold & Porter in Washington. He left private practice to serve in the Justice Department as a Special Assistant U.S. Attorney prosecuting street crime in Washington and later, as part of the Public Integrity Section, prosecuting corrupt federal officials. Richard returned to private practice and was named a partner before taking his current position.

"My work is divided into two categories. First, I read every word of every bill before it gets to the floor. I'm the Speaker's eyes and ears. I'm not just proofreading for bad grammar, I'm looking for unintended—or intended, but hidden—results. In one bill there may be one definition and in another bill an operative term and you'll never see what effect they'll have on the law of the state unless you read them together. Second, I'm working as part of the political process, on a bunch of issues, trying to move concepts into plans, plans into language, and from language to a consensus for final action.

"I arrive at work, spend the whole day going to meetings, come back to the office and think I haven't achieved anything. I used to mark success by billable hours or memos and letters out the door. I don't have those benchmarks now. I talk a lot to people, and those conversations are work. In the legislature, just walking down the hall, you can get a lot done through chance encounters."

The executive branch hires lawyers of its own both to run executive departments and to assist with the legislative and regulatory process. Every major government agency has its own counsel's office. These lawyers may have regulatory enforcement duties, administrative duties, policy-making duties, or a combination of these. And, of course, government executives such as the President hire their own legal counsel.

Finally, there are a host of quasi-governmental legal jobs. These are found in the many institutions sponsored or funded by government. As assistant general counsel of the Smithsonian Institution, Elaine Johnston has a "very broad general practice. The Smithsonian is a lot bigger than people realize. There are fifteen museums, a magazine, research centers around the world, TV and video productions and publications. What I do changes over time depending on the types of problems coming up. Anything from dealing with gifts and bequests, tax issues, contracts, personnel matters, historical preservation issues, and endangered species problems. In law school the issues raised in property class seemed so archaic, not related to life. Law of gifts now makes up a large part of what I do and I love it." Elaine likes the variety in her work. "I deal with curators, historians, museum directors, people who are experts in fields I find interesting. Very little is adversarial. We're trying to avoid legal problems." She also likes the independence of her job, but admits, "I'd much rather be doing what my clients are doing than what I'm doing, even though they need my expertise to do it. Their side is more interesting. I spend more time looking at documents and dealing with technicalities."

At its best, government work provides lawyers with the opportunity to work on cutting-edge legal issues and to influence or implement public policy. Government service also provides the intangible benefits of public service. "One of the things that have been so wonderful about my practice," says Barrie Goldstein, who worked both for the U.S. Justice Department and later for the New York Attorney General's office, "is being able to stand up in court and say, 'Your honor, the Government submits . . .' When you're a government lawyer, you not only represent your client—the state or federal entity that employs you—you also represent the public interest. That's the fundamental difference between private practice and government practice."

Government service also provides reasonable job security, except for political patronage positions. (However, the trend of employee layoffs so popular with corporations in the 1990s has recently spread to government cutbacks as well.)

One outmoded perception is that government lawyers don't work very hard. The hours probably are more predictable in nonpolicy-making and nontrial positions. But for the lawyers in policy-making positions, for public defenders, prosecutors, and others who litigate, the hours as a government lawyer are just as demanding as they are in private practice. One former private firm trial lawyer told me, "I'm working as many or more hours now, but it doesn't seem like it. The day passes so quickly."

The disadvantages of government work include the pay, the bureaucracy, and limited advancement opportunities. You will be paid less in a government job than you could earn in private practice or as an in-house counsel. In some government positions, your independence and ability to effect change may be limited by formalities and red tape. Government lawyers often work with fewer resources than private lawyers. Yvonne Facchina, a senior attorney at the Enforcement Division of the Federal Reserve Board in Washington, D.C., remarked that government support services are more limited than those found in law firms, "so you'd better be good at typing and filing. And there are not enough supplies or equipment. We are desperate for Post-Its!" Finally, in upper-level government legal jobs, your ability to advance, or even to keep your current job, may depend on the fortunes of electoral politics.

Representing the Public Interest

"After spending one and a half years at a private firm, I opted to work in Legal Aid," says Cathy Lesser Mansfield. "I started as a staff attorney for the Urban Indian Law Office of Community Legal Services in Phoenix. The job was incredibly challenging because I had to do a little bit of everything—domestic relations, public benefits, landlord-tenant, and consumer law. It was much more hectic than private practice because I was less insulated and there were more clients than the office could possibly help. Every week we had twenty-five to thirty new cases, but we could only handle about five. At any given time, I was personally handling forty to fifty cases.

"The major difference was my level of autonomy. I was driving the bus. I was responsible for each victory and loss. I had tons of client contact. However, my public interest clients weren't always that participatory. I had several clients who didn't show up for depositions or court appearances. Sometimes I seemed to care more about the cases than the client did. The stakes were more human in my public interest job. I was fighting for child custody or to protect a family from being thrown out on the streets. Consequently, I had great personal satisfaction in my job. Whenever I would hear anyone say that we should help the poor, the sick, or the needy, I would think to myself, Yep. That's what I do."

There are at least two broad categories of nonprofit organizations that employ lawyers. First are the groups, such as state legal services organizations, which provide legal advice to the poor. Second are the wide variety of issue-oriented groups that attempt to affect public policy.

Legal services organizations are sometimes private and sometimes governmental or quasi-governmental organizations. The federal government has for years funded the Legal Services Organization, which provides federal funding to nonprofit organizations representing the poor across the country. Many states and cities have similar groups that are funded both with money from government and by interest earned on client trust funds that otherwise would go to the banks holding those funds. These legal services organizations typically provide landlord-tenant, divorce, and other litigation-oriented services to indigent persons.

There are literally thousands of issue-oriented nonprofit groups, many of which rely on lawyers. Environmental groups such as the Sierra Club and the Natural Resources Defense Council have gained prominence in part through high-profile lawsuits intended to protect the environment. Groups on both sides of the abortion debate have used lawyers and litigation to affect public perceptions and public policy. Lawyers are also active in nonprofit organizations opposed to the death penalty. Even nonprofits that do not engage regularly in litigation hire lawyers as lobbyists, strategists, and policy makers for their groups.

Public interest law allows many lawyers to do what they enjoy. Lawyers working in the public interest work toward achieving public policy goals important to them personally. "I have a lot more control than I did as an associate at a law firm. And I feel like I'm making more of a contribution," says the NOW Legal Defense Fund's Martha Davis, who works on litigation of women's issues and advises NOW local chapters around the country. "I love what I'm doing. It's something I feel committed to." The psychic benefits of making a difference by serving a public cause are important because public interest lawyers are usually poorly paid, often work incredibly hard, and in some cases are subject to job insecurity due to funding uncertainties.

Back to School

Practicing law isn't for everyone. "I couldn't practice law if I fell on it," says Southern Cal professor Charles Whitebread. "If I practiced law, I'd start eating lunch with clients at nine-thirty and I'd keep eating lunch with clients until six-thirty. But I'd have lots of talented guys back at the office who could do the work." Private practice's loss is teaching's gain. Professor Whitebread is one of the most talented classroom lecturers teaching law anywhere, and someone who found his proper place in the law.

Inevitably, many of the brightest law students decide against practicing law and opt, instead, to teach it. For these lawyers, the appeal of law is primarily intellectual. Legal practitioners look at law to determine the permissible boundaries of their clients' activities. In essence, the practice of law amounts to advising clients whether their activities fall within those boundaries and resolving disputes when they don't. Teaching law, in contrast, provides the opportunity not just to teach where those boundaries are. It also permits law professors to think, debate, and write about where legal boundaries ought to be drawn and why.

Sharon Tisher left private practice to teach environmental law to undergraduates at the University of Maine. "It's marvelous being in an academic setting—it's like regaining my youth. There are all kinds of opportunities for intellectual investigation: testifying on environmental legislation, writing law review articles, and participating in faculty workshops. When I left the firm it felt like I'd walked off the face of the earth, but it's been a cinch to retool. What I'm doing now is more interesting than private practice, but doesn't pay as much."

Life in the ivory tower of law school can be very attractive. Many of us think of our time in school as the best years of our lives. Who wouldn't want to continue being around bright, energetic students and to be paid for pondering the great issues of the day? Teaching law is one of the least stressful jobs you can get with a law degree. One law professor recalled how another had described the responsibilities of teaching law: "He said that when he turned his desk chair toward his window, stared outside, and thought, he was earning his entire salary." Not bad work, if you can get it.

Still, the ivory tower has its own pressures. Publish or perish. Heavy teaching loads. Tenure battles. There is some mobility from private practice to teaching, but generally little the other way. (Of course, it may be that law professors are smart enough not to want to practice law.)

Miscellaneous

There are many jobs held by lawyers that don't fit in these broad categories. Jane Lehman worked for several years as a researcher for the National Legal Research Group, a large firm that performs legal research for lawyers around the country. "I helped them with their most difficult and interesting problems—the ones they considered unsolvable. And it was my job to solve them." Now Jane works out of her home for the publications arm of the same company, authoring sections of legal treatises. "The end result of these projects is a published work with my name on it. What I write will be there for thirty years to help others with their legal research. That's really satisfying."

Some of the options that a law degree keeps open are in nonlegal positions. Many corporate CEOs are lawyers. As are many journalists, lobbyists, and politicians. At least one member of the Super Bowl champion San Francisco 49ers is a lawyer.

Why do you find people with law degrees succeeding in so many fields? Professor Charles Whitebread has an answer. "What's made teaching law from 1968 to today so much fun is that most nonscience undergraduates—or at least the best of them—went on to law school. Many of my law students went into business, where they excelled. Law grads are better than others in so many fields, whether they're screenwriters, in communications, or just general businessmen. They're so good because they've competed against the very best in law school. After that, they can handle anything."

One lawyer I spoke to agreed. "The most important thing about law school isn't the law, it's learning to think like a lawyer. Being able to think in analytical and logical terms. Identifying relevant standards in a particular situation, taking the flood of data that comes washing over you and structuring it in a way that has meaning to those relevant standards. The black-letter law is just a means to developing those analytical skills. You can never learn all the law, and when you do they just make more the next day. But someone who's developed lawyerly *skills* can do anything."

Legal Options for Nonlawyers

You don't have to go to law school to work in a law-related job. There are many roles for nonlawyers in and around the legal profession. Perhaps the most visible legal position for nonlawyers is that of paralegal or legal assistant. Legal assistants work directly with lawyers in law firms and corporations. They are not paid as well as lawyers are, and the law puts certain limits on the things they can do (because they aren't licensed, they can't "practice law"). But paralegals play a vital role in the legal profession. They draft contracts, handle real estate closings, assist with income tax preparation, and manage documents in complex litigation. Some paralegals are career professionals. Others just want to get a year or two of experience while deciding whether to go to law school.

Title searchers are one form of specialized paralegal. Title searchers go to the land records for a city or county and research the ownership of particular pieces of property over time. They also can determine whether a bank has a mortgage on the property or whether there are restrictions on how the property can be developed or used. Title searching is sometimes performed by lawyers, but is often performed by nonlawyers who work for law firms, title insurance companies, or title searching firms. You can't buy or sell a house, or even take out a home equity loan, without the help of a title searcher.

Another law-related job is that of jury consultant. The sensational trials of William Kennedy Smith and O. J. Simpson showed how jury consultants can play a vital role in high-stakes trials. Jury consultants help trial lawyers pick jurors that are more likely to be sympathetic to one side or the other. They also assemble mock juries to allow lawyers to try out their arguments in advance of trial to see which arguments work and which witnesses are persuasive. Jury consultants are sometimes lawyers, but often they have psychology or sociology backgrounds.

Court reporters or stenographers are the people you see in a courtroom seated in front of what appears to be a small typewriter. Court reporters take down the words that are spoken at trial or depositions in order to prepare a transcript (and usually also a computer disk) of exactly what was said. Sometimes they also provide video equipment to record proceedings on videotape. Thousands of court reporters are busy taking and transcribing testimony in courts and lawyers' offices every day. "The salaries are decent, the hours are good, and the things you hear are amazing," explained an experienced court reporter with a small reporting firm in Arizona. "I work for an attorney who specializes in personal injury work, and the testimony I transcribe proves that the truth is stranger than fiction."

Legal librarians work in law libraries at law schools, law firms, and corporations. Some law librarians have their law degree, but many studied library science instead. Law librarians do everything that other librarians do—from updating the library's collection of periodicals to indexing the collection to reshelving the books. Some legal librarians do some legal research too. Especially with the rise of computer-based legal research, law librarians have become more involved in certain types of legal research. At my law firm, for example, the law librarians often assist with checking citations in briefs before they are filed in court.

All of these positions are related to the law. All require specialized training. And while a law degree would be helpful in most of these jobs, it is usually not required. If you have an interest in the law, but for whatever reason are not sure that you would like being a lawyer, you should explore these and other law-related jobs as alternatives.

· 11 ·

LEGAL ADVICE

Read a book written by a lawyer, and you're going to get some advice. That's what we do for a living after all, offer advice. Here are my suggestions for how you can continue the process of finding a satisfying career in the law or elsewhere:

1. *Not deciding is a bad decision.* You can drift into law school, having failed to decide to do anything else. You can drift into a legal job, having failed to decide what it is you want to do. And you can drift along doing your legal work. But one day you will wake up and ask how you got where you are. By failing to take control of your destiny you will have made a decision that you are almost sure to regret someday.

An ounce of preparation is worth a pound of cure. Confront yourself to figure out just what it is you want out of a career. Job security, prestige, contribution to the public good, intellectual stimulation, money, the opportunity to create. You can't find what you're looking for if you don't know what it is.

2. *Prepare for surprise.* You think you want to be a lawyer, maybe even a particular kind of lawyer. Whatever your motivation for thinking that now, keep an open mind with regard to other opportunities. In our dynamic economy, new careers are being created constantly. (I remember in the mid-1970s being curious about what a college acquaintance would be doing when I heard he had taken a job with a new company called Home Box Office.) The perfect job for you may not have been created yet—or at least you may not have heard anything about it yet. Don't become so fixated on any job that you lose your vision for what else is possible.

Question your assumptions about the law. We all draw inferences and conclusions from whatever limited information we have about a particular subject at a given time. Have you ever tried to picture what someone looks like from their voice on the telephone? You can often draw a clear mental picture, right? But how often has your picture been accurate when you actually meet that person? You probably have a vision of what it would be like to practice law too. Chances are that your vision of what it will be like to be a lawyer is not completely accurate. Be ready to accept the difference between perception and reality and move on.

3. *Be true to yourself.* You can't become a lawyer—or a banker or an actor or a physician—for anyone but yourself. Listen to advice from others, but when it's time for you to make career decisions, listen only to your inner voice. The pleasure of impressing someone else with what you do is fleeting. The pain of working day after day in a job you deplore is constant. Unless you are true to yourself, to your own interests and desires, you will be making a mistake.

Don't be too quick to trade off a job in which you would do something you enjoy for a job that pays more. In college and law school there seems to be an informal ranking that correlates success with salary, the same way that pro golfers and tennis players are ranked by their earnings on the circuit each year. All too often the assumption is that the "best" job is the one that pays the most. Job satisfaction is harder to quantify than salary, but the best job is the one you enjoy the most.

A big part of being true to yourself is finding and maintaining your own personal balance between your career and the rest of your life. Don't forget the rest of your life, whatever you do. One lawyer who escaped from an overly demanding position did it for his kids. "I felt like I was kissing them on the head before they got up in the morning and patting them on the head in bed when I got home. I wasn't seeing them except when they were asleep. Men and women alike have to stand up and say we want to spend more time with our children. A high-pressure law practice is not at all conducive to parenthood. You know, on their deathbeds, people never say I wish I'd spent more time at the office. I just had to quit. With kids, you blink and they're gone."

Some lawyers have been able to find balance by working part-time. One told me, "I started working part-time when my first child was born. I'd been an associate for about five years. Some people say working part-time in litigation is harder than in corporate, but I didn't find that to be the case. As a corporate lawyer, you're expected to be in the office. As a litigator, you're expected to be out of the office a lot of the time. Still, you have to be good about returning your phone calls. You have to be super responsible and flexible. Both my husband and I worked part-time and covered for each other, so I could work any day of the week if I had to." After working part-time for several years, she made partner—on her own terms.

4. *Cultivate mentors.* Don't be afraid to ask. Law school does not prepare you to practice law. But for what you're able to pick up during your summer jobs or in clinical courses, most of you will not have a clue what to do the first time a client calls you up for advice or the first time you appear before a real judge in a real courtroom. What's more, if you thought you got little feedback in law school, wait until you're at a law firm. (Corporations are generally better at this.) You're left to figure out how you're doing by how much your draft letter to the client was edited before it was sent out or by whether the partner will let you take the next deposition.

Find a mentor. Or as one lawyer I interviewed put it, "Hire yourself a mentor. Find a person who's an outstanding lawyer and who has values similar to your own and make yourself indispensable to him or her." Your mentor should be someone senior to you whom you can talk to freely. Maybe your mentor will be someone you hit it off with while interviewing, or someone you worked for as a summer associate. Maybe it will be someone you work for on your first few projects. Maybe it will be a senior associate working on the same big case you are, whom you get to know on long plane rides and late nights at the client's offices. Maybe it will be another solo with whom you share office space.

One lawyer who found himself in criminal court for the first time also found a mentor there. His client was accused of selling drugs to an undercover police officer. As the district attorney was calling the case, the lawyer turned to a friend who graduated law school a year earlier. "Psst, Alex, what do I say?" "Just tell them to 'hold it open' so you can negotiate with the DA." "Then what?" "Then you go to the negotiation room in the back and work out your deal." At that point the new lawyer turned to his client and said confidently, "Yeah, I had your case held open. Now I gotta negotiate your case in the back. Wait here!"

Ask your mentor to review your first few writing projects before you submit them. Find out what the senior people in your office expect from newer lawyers. Get some advice about the politics of the place. Find out what the lawyers you're working for may not be telling you about perceptions of your strengths and weaknesses.

A mentor can dramatically improve your chances of succeeding in an office by telling you what you won't pick up in any official publications. To get ahead, you must quickly learn the culture of an office and adapt to it. A mentor can act as your advocate in behind-the-scenes meetings that may affect your future prospects with your employer. A mentor may also be able to help you if you decide to move on. It's always helpful to have someone whom you can bounce ideas off of. Someone who can make a few calls for you or give a good reference.

5. *Cut your losses.* We all make mistakes. Even if you've done your homework, you may end up working at a place or in a profession that's just not right for you. If you've tried to work through the problem and it hasn't helped, don't be afraid to admit it. Staying on longer than you should will only compound the error.

But don't jump at the first opportunity that comes along. Start the entire process of career decision making over again. You will have greater knowledge of the working world and perhaps a better perspective on your own needs and desires, but the decisions are not likely to be any easier. Take your time and get it right the second time. A law degree does keep a lot of options open for you. That is not reason enough to go to law school, but it does provide some comfort if you can't stand the practice of law.

6. *Make your own luck.* Better to be lucky than good. How many times have you heard that one? What's often overlooked is how often the good make their own luck. No, you can't control luck, but you can influence it. If you work smart and work hard, you can put yourself in a position to be lucky.

There may be only one opening for a lawyer at the place where you'd really like to work, and dozens of people may be applying. You'll have to be really lucky to get that job, right? So make yourself some luck. Work to figure out exactly what the employer is looking for and retool your résumé to reflect it. Work to discover who the decision maker is, and personalize your application by addressing it to that person. Prepare for your interview by reading all of the publicly available information about that firm or company, and refer to recent developments during your interview. Look up lawyers who already work there in *Martindale-Hubbell* or in a listing of corporate in-house counsel at your local law library so that you can refer to their background and accomplishments. In short, do everything you can to stand out from the pack. This hard work may not get you the job, but it puts you in a position to be lucky.

Throughout your career, you'll face many wonderful opportunities. Make the most of them by creating some luck for yourself.

7. *Keep developing your career.* Things change. To stay on top of your career and to keep happy in what you do, you have to change too. Change your area of concentration, change your job, change your career. As soon as your name appears in *Martindale-Hubbell*, you'll start get-

ting calls from legal recruiters. Headhunters. Offering opportunities. More money. More responsibility. More freedom. Or so they say. Keep an open mind, but remember to question what you're told by anyone who will earn a commission off of your decision.

Many newer lawyers get depressed thinking about doing what they're doing for the rest of their lives. Don't we all. As one of my law professors put it, "Nobody wants to do anything for the rest of their lives. The second you frame it that way, it's over." So don't frame it that way. Forget the rest of your life for a while and get back to a number you're comfortable with—three or four years. You made it through four years of high school, four years of college, and three years of law school. Ask yourself if there's anything you'd rather be doing for the next three or four years or after the next three or four years. If the answer is no, great. You're happier than you think. If the answer is yes, start planning. By breaking your career into bite-sized pieces, you'll allow the rest of your life to take care of itself.

I entered the legal profession without doing many of the things I've suggested you should do. Things worked out for me, and for many others who sort of drifted into law about the time I did. But times have changed. Just since I became a lawyer ten years ago, the profession has become much more competitive, the job market has become incredibly tight, and many purchasers of legal services have become more sophisticated and demanding. All of this means that law will likely be a little less fun and a little more risky for you than it was for me.

But if you develop superb lawyering skills, keep your eyes open to the opportunities around you, and take smart risks, you can do anything you want with your law degree. Anything. So follow your dreams.

IGNORANCE OF THE LAW IS NO EXCUSE

APPENDIX A

LEGAL WRITING

Here are some suggestions for further reading.

S. Bell, for the Young Lawyers Division of the American Bar Association, *Full Disclosure: Do You Really Want to Be a Lawyer?*, Peterson's Guides (2nd ed. 1992), $12.95. Essays by and about lawyers.

R. Bolles, *What Color Is Your Parachute? A Practical Manual for Job Hunters and Career Changers*, Ten Speed Press (1995), $21.95. The classic self-help career manual.

Career Choices for the 90s for Students of Law, Walker & Co. (1990), $8.95. Comparisons of entry-level jobs for new lawyers.

C. Carter and G. June, *Graduating into the Nineties: Getting the Most Out of Your First Job After College*, The Noonday Press (1993), $10.00. Advice about how to handle your first job.

C. Carter, *Majoring in the Rest of Your Life*, The Noonday Press (1990), $9.00. Advice about how to succeed in college and in your future career.

C. Cooper, *The Insider's Guide to the Top Fifteen Law Schools*, Bantam Doubleday Dell (1990), $12.95. Descriptions and evaluations of fifteen law schools.

S. Gillers, ed., *Looking at Law School*, Meridian (1990), $10.00. Essays by law professors about the law school experience and courses at law school.

S. Goldfarb, ed., *Inside the Law Schools: A Guide by Students for Students*, Plume (6th ed. 1993), $12.00. Descriptions of over 100 law schools, based on reports from law students.

J. Gordon, *Law School: A Survivor's Guide*, Harper Perennial (1994), $10.00. Humorous view of law and law school.

Law Services, *So You Want to Be a Lawyer: A Practical Guide to Law as a Career*, Bantam Doubleday Dell (1994), $13.95. Overview of lawyering and law school.

Law Services, *The Official Guide to U.S. Law Schools*, Bantam Doubleday Dell (1994), $18.95. Descriptions and statistics about each of the 176 ABA-approved law schools.

M. Oldman and S. Hamadeh, *The Princeton Review Student Access Guide to America's Top 100 Internships*, Random House (1995), $17.00. Descriptions and prerequisites for various internships, including some in the legal profession.

M. Simenhoff, ed., *My First Year as a Lawyer*, Walker & Company (1994), $9.95. A collection of eighteen true stories about first-year lawyers.

123

United States Government Manual, U.S. Government Printing Office (1994), $23.00. The official handbook of the federal government, containing overviews of government agencies, their purpose and role.

I. Van Tuyl, *The Princeton Review Student Access Guide to the Best Law Schools*, Random House (1994), $20.00. Everything from a history of the American law school, to the LSAT, to statistics and rankings of law schools.

C. Whitebread, *Success in Law School: Exam Taking Techniques*, Harcourt Brace Jovanovich (1989), $10.00. A survival guide to law school exams.

N. M. Yeager, *CareerMap: Deciding What You Want, Getting It and Keeping It!*, John Wiley & Sons (1988), $14.95. An upbeat guide to career planning and decision making.

APPENDIX B

HOW TO FIND A FRIENDLY BAR (ASSOCIATION)

The following is a list of addresses and phone numbers for the American Bar Association and the various state bar associations. Many localities have their own, more focused bar associations. You can usually find them listed in the yellow pages under "Associations" or by asking your state bar association. Most of these organizations can provide information about legal employers in the areas they serve.

Alabama State Bar
415 Dexter Avenue
PO Box 671
Montgomery, Alabama 36101
(334) 269-1515
fax (334) 261-6310

Alaska Bar Association
510 L Street, No. 602
PO Box 100279
Anchorage, Alaska 99510
(907) 272-7469
fax (907) 272-2932

American Bar Association
750 North Lake Shore Drive
Chicago, Illinois 60611
(312) 988-5522
fax (312) 988-5568

State Bar of Arizona
111 West Monroe Street, Suite 1800
Phoenix, Arizona 85003-1742
(602) 252-4804
fax (602) 271-4930

Arkansas Bar Association
400 West Markham
Little Rock, Arkansas 72201
(501) 375-4606
fax (501) 375-4901

State Bar of California
555 Franklin Street
San Francisco, California 94102
(415) 561-8200
fax (415) 561-8305

Colorado Bar Association
1900 Grant Street, Suite 950
Denver, Colorado 80203
(303) 860-1115
fax (303) 894-0821

Connecticut Bar Association
101 Corporate Place
Rocky Hill, Connecticut 06067-1894
(203) 721-0025
fax (203) 257-4125

Delaware Bar Association
1225 North King Street
Wilmington, Delaware 19801-3233
(302) 658-5279
fax (302) 658-5212

District of Columbia Bar
1250 H Street NW
Suite 600
Washington, D.C. 20005-3908
(202) 737-4700
fax (202) 626-3471

Bar Association of the District of
  Columbia
1819 H Street NW
12th Floor
Washington, D.C. 20006-3690
(202) 223-6600
fax (202) 293-3388

The Florida Bar
650 Apalachee Parkway
Tallahassee, Florida 32399-2300
(904) 561-5600
fax (904) 561-5827

State Bar of Georgia
50 Hurt Plaza, Suite 800
Atlanta, Georgia 30303
(404) 527-8700
fax (404) 527-8717

Hawaii State Bar Association
1136 Union Mall
Penthouse One
Honolulu, Hawaii 96813
(808) 537-1868
fax (808) 521-7936

Idaho State Bar
PO Box 895
Boise, Idaho 83701
(208) 334-4500
fax (208) 334-4515

Illinois State Bar Association
424 South Second Street
Springfield, Illinois 62701
(217) 525-1760
fax (217) 525-0712

Indiana State Bar Association
230 East Ohio Street
4th Floor
Indianapolis, Indiana 46204
(317) 639-5465
fax (317) 266-2588

Iowa State Bar Association
521 East Locust
Des Moines, Iowa 50309
(515) 243-3179
fax (515) 243-2511

Kansas Bar Association
1200 S.W. Harrison Street
Topeka, Kansas 66612
(913) 234-5696
fax (913) 234-3813

Kentucky Bar Association
514 West Main Street
Frankfort, Kentucky 40601-1883
(502) 564-3795
fax (502) 564-3225

Louisiana State Bar Association
601 St. Charles Avenue
New Orleans, Louisiana 70130
(504) 566-1600
fax (504) 566-0930

Maine State Bar Association
124 State Street
PO Box 788
Augusta, Maine 04332
(207) 622-7523
fax (207) 623-0083

Maryland State Bar Association
520 West Fayette Street
Baltimore, Maryland 21201
(410) 685-7878
fax (410) 837-0518

Massachusetts Bar Association
20 West Street
Boston, Massachusetts 02111-1218
(617) 542-3602
fax (617) 426-4344

State Bar of Michigan
306 Townsend Street
Lansing, Michigan 48933-2083
(517) 372-9030
fax (517) 482-6248

Minnesota State Bar Association
514 Nicollet Mall
Suite 300
Minneapolis, Minnesota 55402
(612) 333-1183
fax (612) 333-4927

The Mississippi Bar
643 North State Street
Jackson, Mississippi 39201
(601) 948-4471
fax (601) 355-8635

The Missouri Bar
326 Monroe
Jefferson City, Missouri 65102
(314) 635-4128
fax (314) 635-2811

State Bar of Montana
46 North Last Chance Gulch
PO Box 577
Helena, Montana 59624
(406) 442-7660
fax (406) 442-7763

Nebraska State Bar Association
635 South 14th Street
2nd Floor
Lincoln, Nebraska 68501-1809
(402) 475-7091
fax (402) 475-7098

State Bar of Nevada
201 Las Vegas Boulevard South
Suite 200
Las Vegas, Nevada 89101
(702) 382-2200
fax (702) 385-2878

New Hampshire Bar Association
112 Pleasant Street
Concord, New Hampshire 03301
(603) 224-6942
fax (603) 224-2910

New Jersey State Bar Association
New Jersey Law Center
One Constitution Square
New Brunswick, New Jersey 08901-
1500
(908) 249-5000
fax (908) 249-2815

State Bar of New Mexico
121 Tijeras Street NE
Albuquerque, New Mexico 87102
(505) 842-6132
fax (505) 843-8765

New York State Bar Association
One Elk Street
Albany, New York 12207
(518) 463-3200
fax (518) 463-4276

North Carolina State Bar
208 Fayetteville Street Mall
Raleigh, North Carolina 27611
(919) 828-4620
fax (919) 821-9168

North Carolina Bar Association
8000 Weston Parkway
PO Box 3688
Cary, North Carolina 27519-3688
(919) 677-0561
fax (919) 677-0761

State Bar Association of North Dakota
515½ East Broadway
Bismarck, North Dakota 58502
(701) 255-1404
fax (701) 224-1621

Ohio State Bar Association
1700 Lake Shore Drive
PO Box 16562
Columbus, Ohio 43216-0562
(614) 487-2050
fax (614) 487-1008

Oklahoma Bar Association
1901 North Lincoln
Oklahoma City, Oklahoma 73105
(405) 524-2365
fax (405) 524-1115

Oregon State Bar
5200 Southwest Meadows Road
PO Box 1689
Lake Oswego, Oregon 97035
(503) 620-0222
fax (503) 684-1366

Pennsylvania Bar Association
100 South Street
PO Box 186
Harrisburg, Pennsylvania 17108
(717) 238-6715
fax (717) 238-1204

Puerto Rico Bar Association
PO Box 1900
San Juan, Puerto Rico 00902
(809) 721-3358
fax (809) 725-0330

Rhode Island Bar Association
115 Cedar Street
Providence, Rhode Island 02903
(401) 421-5740
fax (401) 421-2703

South Carolina Bar
950 Taylor Street
PO Box 608
Columbia, South Carolina 29202
(803) 799-6653
fax (803) 799-4118

State Bar of South Dakota
222 East Capitol
Pierre, South Dakota 57501
(605) 224-7554
fax (605) 224-0282

Tennessee Bar Association
3622 Westend Avenue
Nashville, Tennessee 37205
(615) 383-7421
fax (615) 297-8058

State Bar of Texas
1414 Colorado
PO Box 12487
Austin, Texas 78711-2487
(512) 463-1400
fax (512) 463-1475

Utah State Bar
645 South 200 East
Suite 310
Salt Lake City, Utah 84111
(801) 531-9077
fax (801) 531-0660

Vermont Bar Association
PO Box 100
Montpelier, Vermont 05601
(802) 223-2020
fax (802) 223-1573

Virginia State Bar
707 East Main Street
Suite 1500
Richmond, Virginia 23219-2803
(804) 775-0500
fax (804) 775-0501

Virginia Bar Association
701 East Franklin Street
Suite 1120
Richmond, Virginia 23219
(804) 644-0041
fax (804) 644-0052

Virgin Islands Bar Association
PO Box 4108
Christiansted, Virgin Islands 00822
(809) 778-7497
fax (809) 778-7497

Washington State Bar Association
500 Westin Building
2001 Sixth Avenue
Seattle, Washington 98121-2599
(206) 727-8200
fax (206) 727-8320

West Virginia State Bar
2006 Kanawha Boulevard East
Charleston, West Virginia 25311
(304) 558-2456
fax (304) 558-2467

State Bar of Wisconsin
402 West Wilson Street
PO Box 7158
Madison, Wisconsin 53707-7158
(608) 257-3838
fax (608) 257-5502

Wyoming State Bar
500 Randall Avenue
PO Box 109
Cheyenne, Wyoming 82003-0109
(307) 632-9061
fax (307) 632-3737

APPENDIX C

LEGAL PERSONALITY

Many school career guidance centers and professional career consultants use a personality assessment tool, the Myers-Briggs Type Indicator® (MBTI), to inventory personality traits in four general areas: how you like to interact with others, how you like to acquire information, how you make decisions, and how you plan and implement decisions.

Overview
The Myers-Briggs Type Indicator is designed to give you an idea of your personality "type." Personalities are grouped by preferences for: (1) Extroversion ("E") or Introversion ("I"); (2) Sensing ("S") or Intuition ("N"); (3) Thinking ("T") or Feeling ("F"); and (4) Judging ("J") or perceiving ("P"). Let's look at what each set of preferences means.

1. Extroversion/Introversion ("E/I")
The first MBTI scale assesses how you deal with others. An extrovert is stimulated by spending time interacting with the external world of people, places, and events. An introvert is energized by focusing on the interior world of ideas and feelings. Extroverts are outgoing, in contrast to the more reserved introvert. In the extreme, extroverts will enjoy themselves at a large party, even though they don't know more than a few people there, while introverts would rather be alone pursuing creative or cognitive activities, such as reading, writing, or drawing.

As a lawyer, an introvert will prefer solo assignments that require research, writing, and thinking as opposed to "networking" to bring in new clients, socializing with their colleagues to ensure that they won't be overlooked during the partnership vote, or trial work which necessitates putting on a show for the jury. Extroverts are likely to enjoy the networking and socializing parts of lawyering, as well as the public aspect of jury trials, oral arguments and negotiating sessions. But they may not enjoy researching and drafting legal memoranda because such activities are so solitary.

2. Sensing/Intuition ("S/N")
The second MBTI scale assesses how you collect information. If you prefer to rely on your five senses, rather than your gut, then you prefer sensing to intui-

tion. The characteristics of someone who prefers sensing to intuition include pragmatism, an ability to retain facts, a detail orientation, and precision.

Intuitives collect information by focusing on more than just raw data. They look for underlying meanings and future implications. They are often verbal, and can devise creative strategies and solutions. To compare the sensing with intuitive preference types, imagine a friend describing a book to you. A sensing type would be able to tell you the title and author, and the essential facts of the plot. An intuitive might not remember the details, but could relate the general tone, story, and what meaning the book has for those who read it.

A sensing lawyer will do well with matters that require attention to fact. The intuitives will excel at developing innovative strategies for resolving conflict or presenting legal argument. They will also be good at focusing on the big picture, while the sensers will be good at the detail.

3. Thinking/Feeling ("T/F")

The third category that the MBTI measures is how you make decisions. A thinking type will rely on objective facts and perceptions to make judgments. A person who is categorized as a feeling type will utilize his or her own morals and values, in addition to facts, when making judgments. The feeling label is not meant to imply that a person is an emotional decision maker. Both types are rational decision makers, but use different tools to decide issues.

Decision making is one of the primary functions of an attorney. For the most part, the law and the facts of a case determine outcome, rather than what is morally "right" or "wrong." That is because the law is based on "past precedent" (rules developed in earlier cases), instead of the attorney's or judge's personal standards of what is fair. As Scott Turow, lawyer and author of *Presumed Innocent* and *One L* has written:

> A lawyer may do his job very well, but he does not set the moral agenda. The ends are established by the client, not the attorney. It is the lawyer's obligation to carry those goals forward, within the limits of law and ethics. It is his job to be a competent professional, to do well, without regard to whether he is doing good.

Because of this system, the ability to make decisions for clients by examining the facts and legal rules objectively is an asset for any attorney. A person who makes a decision based upon his or her own view of equity may often be frustrated and may not make realistic assessments of situations.

4. Judging/Perceiving ("J/P")

The fourth and final category that the MBTI rates is how you plan and implement decisions on a day-to-day basis. A judging person prefers structure and organization. Such a person likes to resolve issues. A person with a preference for perceiving, on the other hand, likes flexibility and does not mind leaving decisions open or changing his or her mind if the facts warrant it. The judging type seeks closure and control; the perceiver seeks to keep options open to ensure complete understanding.

An attorney who has a strong preference for judging will have a tendency to see issues in black and white, and will make decisions in an orderly, timely manner. Sometimes facts trickle in slowly, and dramatically alter the legal picture, requiring a change in strategy. A judging person may have a hard time adapting to such developments.

A lawyer who has a strong preference for perceiving will enjoy collecting the facts, and will be able to adapt to new information. However, a perceiver may plan and implement decisions in a disorganized manner or, worse yet, may procrastinate about important decisions.

What Does It All Mean?

Once you figure out how to classify yourself in each of these four categories, you can put the initials together to determine your type. ESTJ, ENFJ, INFJ, and so on. According to Susan Bell and Lawrence Richard's "Anatomy of a Lawyer" in *Full Disclosure: Do You Really Want to Be a Lawyer?* (American Bar Association, 2nd ed. 1992), the most common types of lawyers are ISTJs, ESTJs, ENTJs and ENTPs. Those who prefer to make decisions from a "thinking," rather than a "feeling" perspective, are more likely to be attorneys. Only 35% of lawyers are "feeling" types. This indicates that a person who prefers to inject personal standards and values to make decisions may not be satisfied practicing law.

If this type of personality testing interests you, or if you think it might stimulate you to think more clearly about whether you'd enjoy a career in law, visit your career planning office for more information. Chances are, someone there can test your legal personality.